Career
Academies

David Stern
Marilyn Raby
Charles Dayton

Career Academies

Partnerships for Reconstructing American High Schools

Jossey-Bass Publishers · San Francisco

For sales outside the United States, contact Maxwell Macmillan International Publishing Group, 866 Third Avenue, New York, New York 10022.

Manufactured in the United States of America

The paper used in this book is acid-free and meets the State of California requirements for recycled paper (50 percent recycled waste, including 10 percent postconsumer waste), which are the strictest guidelines for recycled paper currently in use in the United States.

10% POST
CONSUMER
WASTE

Library of Congress Cataloging-in-Publication Data

Stern, David, date.
   Career academies : partnerships for reconstructing American high schools / David Stern, Marilyn Raby, Charles Dayton.
     p.   cm. — (The Jossey-Bass education series)
   Includes bibliographical references.
   ISBN 1-55542-488-0
   1. Career education—Case studies. 2. Career education—California—Case studies. 3. Education, Cooperative—Case studies.
4. Education, Cooperative—California—Case studies. I. Raby, Marilyn, date. II. Dayton, Charles, date. III. Title.
IV. Series
LC1037.6.C2S74   1992
370.11'3'09794—dc20   92—21021
                                    CIP

FIRST EDITION
HB Printing   10 9 8 7 6 5 4 3 2 1   *Code 9288*

The Jossey-Bass
Education Series

Contents

Part Three: The Future

Preface

❧ ○ ❧

Career academies have been proliferating in American high schools. The first few started in Philadelphia during the late 1960s and 1970s. In the early 1980s several more appeared in California and New York City. The State of California and the National Academy Foundation separately sponsored dozens of new academies in the late 1980s and early 1990s. Others are springing up independently. Most of the approximately 150 career academies now in existence have originated within the past five years. The academies offer solutions to some all-too-familiar problems in high schools, where students are chronically apathetic and sometimes hostile, test scores remain low, and employers and colleges alike complain about the poor preparation of graduates.

These problems are not new. Since the American high school took its present form early in this century, dissatisfaction and reform have swelled in recurrent waves, generated by basic flaws in the institution's design. That design, as most of us who work in high schools know, isolates schools from the adult world. They try to teach subject matter detached from its practical context. College-bound students take courses with relatively strong academic rigor but little direct application to tasks outside the classroom, while other students may find some practical relevance in their courses without much rigor or coherence. Grades do not motivate most students to study hard—on the contrary, awarding grades entirely on the basis of individual performance creates a conflict for many students, who are afraid of becoming unpopular with their peers if their grades are too high.

Career Academies describes a way to improve students' motivation and performance by creating a new kind of high school experience for them. This is the first book that attempts to give a comprehensive account of what career academies are, how they work, and what it takes to start and maintain one. The purpose of the book is to satisfy the growing interest in career academies as an option for reconstructing American high schools.

Combining Rigor and Relevance

Career academies are schools-within-schools. Most of them span the last two or three years of high school, but some cover all four years. The curriculum simultaneously trains students in an occupational field and prepares them for college. This appeals to students' practical interests but does not limit their future careers, as vocational programs in high schools often have done. Among the more frequent curricular themes are business, computers, electronics, finance, health occupations, public service, and travel and tourism. These themes encompass a set of career options ranging from jobs that require no postsecondary education to professions that require advanced degrees. The curriculum keeps students' options open by providing courses required for college admission while demonstrating the immediate relevance of academic subject matter to an occupational field.

In addition to the focused course of study, many academies arrange summer employment for students after their junior year and part-time jobs during the senior year, in the same career areas that they are studying. Some academies also recruit adults who work in those areas to serve as volunteer mentors for individual students. These experiences help strengthen the connection in students' minds between their coursework and the world outside school.

Career academies can be described as a set of partnerships. On an institutional level, schools enter into partnerships with local employers to help formulate curricula and to provide speakers, field trips, mentors, and jobs for students. Within the career academy itself, teachers work as partners to coordinate the curriculum and in particular to integrate instruction in academic and vocational subjects. This enables the academy to accommodate a wide range of students, from the college-bound to would-be dropouts, and prevents the program from becoming either an elite enclave or a dumping ground. Each academy teacher can relate lessons to what students are learning in other academy classes. As a result, students have the sense that they are not just taking a disconnected set of arbitrary classes but instead are studying the real world from different angles. Teachers also reach out to form partnerships with parents; when students apply to the program, most academies require that parents become involved from the outset by attending meetings or interviews with their children.

Collaborations among teachers, employers, and parents support the most fundamental partnerships—those involving the students. Keeping students together with the same teachers for more than one year in a small, school-within-a-school setting develops deeper communication, trust, and commitment, which enables students and teachers to become partners rather than adversaries. Likewise, personal contacts with local employers lay the groundwork for academy students to have more worthwhile work experiences than high school students usually find in their part-time jobs. Most important, the students' positive feeling of membership in the academy community can transform the peer group from a source of opposition against academic achievement to a source of support for it. When school offers teenagers the means to deal productively with an issue as vital as finding their place in the world of work, they can shed the resistant, irresponsible posture they are otherwise apt to assume. In short, career academies help young people grow up.

Evaluations of career academies have found positive results. Academies evidently have helped students improve their attendance, grades, and course completion rate. They have encouraged would-be dropouts to finish high school and at the same time have enabled graduates to attend college. The model has also proven to be replicable in new locations. Replication is not simple, however, and poor implementation cannot be expected to yield positive results.

Overview of the Contents

Part One of the book gives an overview of the dilemmas and circumstances that gave birth to career academies. In Chapter One we discuss some of the persistent problems in American high schools. In particular, we address the questions of how students can maintain interest in academic subjects when school is cut off from the adult world, and how students can prepare for both work and further education without creating an invidious system of tracking. In Chapter Two we present the career academy model in detail and explain how it is designed to address these problems. Chapter Three covers the evolution of career academies in Philadelphia and California and describes the nationwide network sponsored by the National Academy Foundation. The results of several evaluations of academies are summarized in Chapter Four.

Part Two explains how to create a career academy based on the California model, which is intended for a broad range of students. Chapter Five lays out the tasks involved in starting an academy, lists potential problems, and offers some principles for guidance when difficulties arise. Chapter Six focuses on procedures for building the crucial partnership between schools and employers. Portraits of academy programs in four California school districts are presented in Chapter Seven. These illustrate how implementation of the model can vary in accordance with local resources and opportunities. One district may make particular contributions in developing integrated curriculum, another in providing high-quality work experiences for students, a third in recruiting mentors, and a fourth in connecting academies to earlier and later phases of schooling.

Finally, in Part Three we consider the future. In Chapter Eight we highlight the Carl D. Perkins Act of 1990, which provides some support for starting and maintaining career academies. The act requires that federal funds for vocational education be spent on programs that integrate academic and vocational instruction and promotes "tech prep" programs that combine the last two years of high school with the first two years of college. We also show how career academies are consonant with other contemporary educational reforms, including the effort to build collaboration between schools and employers and the movement to give parents and students greater choice among school programs. Whether in their current form of school-within-a-school or integrated into the school as a whole, career academies provide a viable model for reconstructing American high schools.

Purpose and Audience

Career Academies is intended to provide useful guidance for teachers, administrators, school boards, employers, citizens, interest groups, foundations, and state and federal policy makers who are trying to reshape the American high school. These readers will be interested in the detailed descriptions of the academy model and in the practical advice and case histories that provide guidelines for starting an academy.

The book is also meant to serve as a reference for scholars, researchers, policy analysts, and others who seek information about career academies. For them, the book compiles information, including the history of existing programs and evaluation results, that has not been previously assembled in one place. It also places career academies in the context of other research and policy analysis.

Background

Of the three of us, Marilyn Raby was the first to become involved with career academies. In 1981 she was the school district official in charge of starting two Peninsula Academies in the Sequoia Union High School District near San Francisco. Later she provided leadership in founding two more academies in her district and has also helped other districts with their academy programs. Charles Dayton began his work with these programs in 1982 as director of business involvement for the Peninsula Academies; since then, he has provided consultation and technical assistance to many school districts and coordinated a group of veteran academy teachers and administrators who have helped spread the model throughout California. David Stern collaborated with Dayton in evaluating the first set of replications, co-authored a series of articles, and has worked with several academies on curriculum development.

David Stern initiated the writing of this book, drafted Chapters One, Four, and Eight, and served as general editor. Marilyn Raby had primary responsibility for Chapter Five, Charles Dayton for Chapters Two and Six. All three contributed to Chapters Three and Seven.

Acknowledgments

This book would not have been possible without the dedication of numerous individuals—teachers, administrators, employees of cooperating companies, and others—who have worked hard to establish career academies as a means to provide a better life for high school students. We refrain from mentioning particular names here only because to name some would be unfair to dozens of others who have also made outstanding contributions. Their altruism, creativity, and persistence have been sometimes heroic and often unrecognized. We can only hope that what we have written does justice to their work.

August 1992

DAVID STERN
Berkeley, California

MARILYN RABY
Redwood City, California

CHARLES DAYTON
Nevada City, California

The Authors

~=⊂ ◯ ⊃=~

DAVID STERN is professor of education at the University of California, Berkeley. He received his A.B. degree (1966) from Harvard University in social relations, his M.S. degree (1968) from the Massachusetts Institute of Technology (MIT) in city planning, and his Ph.D. degree (1972) from MIT in economics and urban studies.

Stern's primary research activities have been in the economics of education—including efficiency and equity in the allocation of school resources, and connections between schooling and labor markets. In recent years, his main interest has been in how learning and work complement or conflict with each other both for working students and for employed adults. His books include *Managing Human Resources: The Art of Full Employment* (1982), *Adolescence and Work: Influences of Social Structure, Labor Markets, and Culture* (1989, coedited with D. Eichorn), and *Market Failure in Training? New Economic Analysis and Evidence on Training of Adult Employees* (1991, coedited with J. Ritzen).

MARILYN RABY is director of curriculum services in the Sequoia Union High School District (Redwood City, California), where she is also project director of the federally funded Partnership Academies demonstration sites. She received her B.S. degree (1958) from Boston University in science education, her M.S. degree (1974) from San Jose State University in science education, and her Ed.D. degree (1989) from Nova University in education administration.

Raby was director of the original Peninsula Academies in California, where she was responsible for managing the development of the academies program from its inception to the point at which its demonstrated effectiveness prompted the California legislature to provide funding for its replication throughout the state. She has written several articles and given numerous presentations about the program. Raby has served on the California State Department of Education's High School Task Force, the Educational Options Advisory Committee, and the Task Force for Dropout Prevention.

CHARLES DAYTON is an educational consultant with Foothill Associates in Nevada City, California. He received his B.A. degree (1966) from the State University of New York, Binghamton, in English, his M.A. degree (1968) from Syracuse University in English, and a second M.A. degree (1979) from San Jose State University in psychology.

Dayton's main work has been related to improving the school-to-work transition for at-risk high school students. From 1972 to 1984 he was a research scientist at the American Institutes for Research in Palo Alto, California; since 1984 he has worked privately for various clients, including the U.S. Department of Education, the California Department of Education, and several private foundations. He coordinated the business involvement of the original Peninsula Academies during their formative period, directed the evaluation of the first set of academy replications, and currently coordinates a statewide technical assistance group for the California Partnership Academies. Dayton has studied, written, and published extensively in the field of school-business partnerships and has sought ways to improve the preparation of young people for the changing needs of the twenty-first century workforce.

Career Academies

Part One:

New Directions for High Schools

ONE

—⚞ ○ ⚟—

High School:
Demand for a New Design

American high schools are under fire. They are criticized because too few students achieve academic excellence or job readiness. Dropout rates are too high, while many students who do stay in school lack motivation.

Especially harsh criticism has recently been directed at the preparation of students who enter the workforce without going to college. For example, the influential report *America's Choice: High Skills or Low Wages!* bluntly charged: "America invests little in its front-line workforce. We do not expect much from them in school. . . . The educational performance of those students who become front-line workers in this country is well below the average performance of their counterparts in some newly industrializing low wage countries. Our front-line workers will not be able to compete in the economic arena because they are increasingly unable to compete in the educational arena. They are fast becoming unemployable at American wage levels. In our expectations for young people, the resources that we devote to them and the rewards for performance that we give them, our whole system conspires to produce minimal educational effort or achievement among our students who are not college bound" (National Center on Education and the Economy, 1990, p. 43).

3

College-bound students are not doing very well, either. Average scores on Scholastic Aptitude Tests (SATs) given to college applicants declined steadily throughout the late 1960s and 1970s, recovered weakly in the early 1980s, but then continued their decline (Ogle, Alsalam, and Rogers, 1991, p. 40), and verbal scores sank to an all-time low in 1991.

Employers and college professors agree that current high school graduates lack functional literacy and problem-solving ability and that they are poorly prepared for either work or higher education, according to a 1991 Harris poll. Employers reported that they had to turn down five of every six young people who applied for a job. Among the higher educators, 77 percent judged that recent high school graduates lacked discipline in their work habits, and 74 percent felt that they did not have a "capacity to concentrate on their studies over an extended period of time" (Harris, 1991, p. A3).

Critics link poor performance by students to weaknesses in curriculum and instruction. Some claim that conventional methods for teaching academic subjects are sterile and useless. Others point to traditional vocational instruction as being outdated and second-rate. Many agree that the general track—comprised of students who are preparing neither for college nor for a particular occupation—is unfocused and unproductive. Conventional curriculum and instruction appear especially ineffective in low-income and minority communities, where dropout rates remain alarmingly high.

Dissatisfaction with high schools is nothing new. For most of this century, American high schools have been struggling with certain dilemmas that are built into their present design. Resolving the dilemmas and improving students' performance requires nothing less than redesigning the high school. Essential features of that redesign are present in the Academy model that is the subject of this book.

High School Dilemmas

Since the early part of this century, when the proportion of young people attending high school increased dramatically and the institution took its present form, a set of difficult dilemmas has created chronic controversy (for example, see Grubb, 1989).

School Versus the Real World

One inherent contradiction is that high schools are supposed to prepare students to assume adult responsibilities, including work, but at the same time schools are also designed to keep students away from the adult world.

Compulsory schooling, restrictions on child labor, and minimum-wage laws all were intended to shelter children from unsafe and unhealthy working conditions and at the same time to prevent children from glutting the labor market. These laws have succeeded in taking students out of the labor market during much of the school day, but they have created the problem of how to get them back into it. Unlike Germany and other countries with well-developed apprenticeship systems for teenagers, the United States lacks effective procedures to help young people make the transition from school to work.

Separation of school from the real world lends a certain artificiality to school activities, and students know it. School-work seldom has any consequences to anyone other than the students themselves. Even for students it often makes no difference. For instance, when students apply for jobs, employers seldom ask to see their high school grades (Bishop, 1989b; Rosenbaum, 1989). In contrast, high school students in Japan have a real incentive to get good grades because the schools select students with good grades to nominate for job interviews with local employers (Rosenbaum and Kariya, 1991). Students in the United States presumably would care more about high school if their performance really mattered.

Since little is at stake beyond teachers' approval, students tend not to encourage one another's academic efforts. "Nerds" are not popular. Students who turn in their homework, volunteer correct answers or constructive comments in class, and score well on exams make other students look bad.

The peer culture in high schools undermines academic achievement. Few students feel a positive sense of membership in a learning community (Newmann, 1991).

Students' indifference wears out teachers, too. Confined to a classroom for day after day of fifty-minute periods, 150 students a day, high school teachers can lose hope of inspiring students to excel (Sizer, 1984). There are teachers who persist in trying to teach because they like the students or the subject or both. But the existing configuration of the high school, and the resulting artificiality of classroom life, typically do not bring out the best in teachers.

"Covering the Material" Versus Learning in Context

The main exception to the general lack of motivation among high school students is exhibited by those who seek admission to competitive four-year colleges. For them, taking the right courses and getting good grades do count.

Moreover, success in winning admission to good colleges matters not only to the students involved but also to the reputations of their high schools. Getting students into good colleges is so important for high schools that college admission requirements have enormous influence on the structure of the high school's entire curriculum. In most high schools, teachers belong to departments defined by academic disciplines, such as English, mathematics, science, and foreign languages. In some schools, science may be broken into departments of physics, chemistry, biology, and earth science. Some foreign languages may also comprise separate departments. Within a department, a few teachers have the privilege of teaching relatively prestigious advanced courses for students competing to enter good colleges. The rest bear the responsibility of instructing less advanced students in such nondescript subjects as "general math" or "English 2," which are often remedial courses or watered-down versions of the college prep courses.

The hegemony of college entrance requirements creates another dilemma. High schools must offer certain courses because colleges require them as prerequisites. But courses designed mainly to "cover material" required for other courses in the future are seriously limited in their ability to arouse students' authentic curiosity. They cannot allow students to go off on long tangents or go deeply into particular issues, even if these departures from the syllabus are interesting and instructive for students. Commitment to qualifying students for future courses means sacrificing some opportunity for spontaneous inquiry in the present. Rather than engaging students in active inquiry, such courses place students in a more passive role (Goodlad, 1984).

Fragmenting human knowledge into separate academic disciplines runs the risk of reducing it to a pile of "inert facts," in Whitehead's (1929) phrase. One of the leading academicians of this century, Whitehead urged educators to nurture students' spontaneous, active inquiry into their own real concerns: "Whatever interest attaches to your subject-matter must be evoked here and now; whatever powers you are strengthening in the pupil, must be exercised here and now; whatever possibilities of mental life your teaching should impart, must be exhibited here and now. That is the golden rule of education" (p. 18).

Whitehead defined education as "the acquisition of the art of the utilization of knowledge" (p. 16). This emphasis on the importance of learning in the context of real application and problem solving has been strongly reaffirmed by contemporary researchers in psychology, anthropology, sociolinguistics, and related disciplines who have come together under the banner of cognitive science. They speak with a remarkable degree of consensus about the importance of "situated" learning (Brown, Collins, and Duguid, 1989; see also Resnick, 1987a, 1987b; Raizen, 1989; Lave and Wenger, 1991). The essential idea is that the knowledge and skills required for problem solving are best acquired in an authentic problem-solving context. Abstract knowledge and algorithmic skills acquired in artificial classroom settings often do not transfer to practical situations. The cognitive scientists have now produced a body of empirical evidence that supports this philosophical belief in the value of learning by doing. It implies that the school curriculum should be constructed around immediate, practical problems. In addition to satisfying formal course prerequisites for college, students should also learn to use the information and skills they are acquiring.

The message of Whitehead and the cognitive scientists is now being translated into public policy, especially as it applies to education for work. The U.S. Department of Labor's Secretary's Commission on Achieving Necessary Skills (SCANS) has proclaimed that "good jobs depend on people who can put knowledge to work" (1991, p. v). Therefore, the commission concluded, "We believe, after examining the findings of cognitive science, that the most effective way of learning skills is 'in context,' placing learning objectives within a real environment rather than insisting that students first learn in the abstract what they will be expected to apply" (p. xv). At present, high school students lack sufficient opportunity to learn in the context of real problem solving. Accordingly, in group interviews SCANS found that "the sense that students clearly distinguish between what goes on in their classrooms and what goes on in the 'real world' was palpable" (p. 5). To make school real, "SCANS suggests three principles from cognitive science:

- Students do not need to learn basic skills before they learn problem-solving skills. The two go together. They are not sequential but mutually reinforcing.
- Learning should be reoriented away from mere mastery of information and toward encouraging students to recognize and solve problems.
- Real know-how—foundation and competencies—cannot be taught in isolation; students need practice in the application of these skills" (p. 19).

SCANS has formulated a set of five common competencies that are used to some extent in all jobs: allocating resources, dealing with people, finding information, understanding systems, and using technology. Development of these competencies rests on a foundation of basic skills (the three Rs), thinking skills, and personal qualities. This formulation of what work requires of schools goes well beyond a set of standard courses. It is intended to "span the chasm between schools and the workplace" (p. xv) by defining competence in a real-world context.

One set of high school classrooms that have in fact practiced learning by doing are the shops and laboratories for vocational education. Traditionally, vocational classes have produced real goods and services for sale or of use to people other than the students involved. They have run restaurants and retail stores, grown crops and raised livestock, built houses, repaired cars, and operated child-care centers, among other enterprises. Many vocational students have also been placed in paid jobs outside the school through cooperative education agreements. There they follow written training plans designed to let them apply and extend what they have learned in the classroom. These various forms of school-supervised work experience provide real contexts for students to learn work-related problem solving. They exemplify education as Whitehead defined it.

In spite of its admirable hands-on approach, vocational education has not escaped criticism. Research on its effectiveness in helping students obtain jobs has produced mixed results (National Institute of Education, 1981; Psacharopoulos, 1987; Bishop, 1989a). Even more damaging have been recent complaints from some employers. Historically, business groups were consistent advocates for starting, and then maintaining, vocational education as a separate curriculum (Lazerson and Grubb, 1974). During the 1980s, however, key business spokespersons began to issue surprisingly sharp criticism of vocational education (National Academy of Sciences, 1984; Committee for Economic Development, 1985; Kearns and Doyle, 1988). The major theme in these new critiques was that students who took a lot of vocational courses in high school were not learning the basic academic skills—in reading, writing, math, science—deemed necessary for the workplace of today and tomorrow. Academic subjects should have absolute priority, the critics said. Competence in basic academic subjects should be assured before students are allowed to enroll in vocational courses.

The Problem of Tracking

These complaints about vocational education point to another dilemma for American high schools. The schools are supposed to be meritocratic, providing equal opportunity for all students. But this is difficult, because some children start school better prepared for the kinds of tasks they will encounter there. Schools respond by providing different kinds of instruction for students who are perceived to differ in academic ability. By the time students reach high school they are often sorted into separate classes by ability, with the more demanding classes leading to college. Classes for students deemed "non–college-bound" tend to be stigmatized as second-rate (Gamoran and Berends, 1987). In particular, traditional vocational education, which has been defined by federal law as preparation for occupations not ordinarily requiring a baccalaureate or advanced degree, has suffered this stigma. Many ambitious students and their parents have avoided such classes, thus perpetuating their bad reputation.

African American and Hispanic students tend to be underrepresented in the college prep classes (Oakes, 1983, 1985). Students who are relegated to classes for the non–college-bound may well feel that the school has no serious interest in them. The fact that minority students are more likely to be enrolled in such classes contributes to their greater likelihood of dropping out before they graduate from high school (Ogle, Alsalam, and Rogers, 1991, p. 28; Gamoran and Mare, 1989). If they do graduate from high school, African Americans and Hispanics are only about half as likely as whites to go on to complete four years of college (Alsalam and Rogers, 1991, p. 34). These differential outcomes by race and ethnicity illustrate that students' backgrounds still have considerable influence on their likelihood of success in school.

Rigor and Relevance

Differentiating the high school curriculum into classes for the college-bound and the presumed non–college-bound is harmful not only because it helps perpetuate racial and ethnic differences in social status but also because it creates a false dichotomy between rigor and relevance. College prep classes are more rigorous. They require students to assimilate more information, manipulate more abstract concepts, and perform more complex calculations. But, as Whitehead and contemporary cognitive scientists have argued, this tends to be inert knowledge, which students often cannot apply to practical problems. In contrast, vocational classes are more relevant to life experience, often situating instruction in the context of real work. Some classes in the general track, such as consumer math, are also designed to be relevant to students' practical concerns. The vocational and general classes, however, are usually less rigorous than college prep classes. Lack of rigor in the general track was the chief complaint in *A Nation at Risk* (National Commission on Excellence on Education, 1983). In vocational education, lack of academic rigor prompted the criticism by employers we have already mentioned.

All students could stand to gain by abandoning this traditional division. Students in classes that are already relatively rigorous could understand and retain more if they had more opportunities to relate what they are taught to real-world applications. Students in less rigorous classes could benefit from additional academic skill and knowledge. For this reason, the 1990 amendments to the Carl D. Perkins Vocational and Applied Technology Education Act (U.S. Congress, 1990), which reauthorized federal support for vocational education, now require that the basic grant be spent on "programs that integrate academic and vocational education . . . through coherent sequences of courses so that students achieve both academic and occupational competencies" (section 235). Such integration is an essential feature of the Academy programs described in this book. The amended Perkins Act and the development of academies are responses to the same dilemmas inherent in the present design of the American high school.

How Career Academies Confront the Dilemmas

The essential idea of the academies discussed here is to organize the core curriculum of the high school around a career-related theme. Local employers are involved in helping design the curriculum, offering internships and summer jobs, and providing mentors. This explicit connection between school and the world outside appeals to students' practical interest in making a living, and for students who do not attend college the academy program provides preparation for the labor market. Students enroll by choice, and this by itself is good for motivation.

By including a sufficiently rigorous set of academic courses, the program also preserves students' option of attending college. Courses in academic subjects include material specifically related to the academy's career theme, which makes them more interesting. Students' interest is further aroused by immediate connections between the program and the real world. Employers' representatives come to the school to speak, and students take trips to workplaces. Adults working in the field serve as mentors for students, introducing them to settings in which they might work and helping them plan their careers. Students also have paid jobs, monitored by the school, in which they can practice and improve on what they have learned in the classroom.

These features make school more real for students, since their schoolwork now has more evident consequences. The design of the academy makes it unnecessary to sort students into college-bound and non–college-bound tracks. This avoids demoralizing students who might otherwise be placed in a slow class. At the same time, the academy can improve students' academic achievement because it combines relevance with rigor.

Finally, a relatively intimate school-within-a-school structure helps create a peer culture in which students encourage rather than undermine one another's academic efforts. A small group of teachers work as a team, coordinating the curriculum and building a community with students around their shared interests. Chapter Two describes these and other elements of the academy model in greater detail.

TWO

The Career Academy Model

This chapter describes what we mean by a career academy. Our experience has been with the California version of the model, and the discussion here is based mainly on that experience. However, we have also noted where other career academies differ from the California Partnership Academy model. The purpose here is to give a concise but reasonably complete description of what most career academies have in common.

Defining Characteristics

While there is variation both within the individual California Partnership Academies and elsewhere, by customary practice a career academy has several defining characteristics:

- It is a school-within-a-school for grades 11 through 12, 10 through 12, or 9 through 12, run by a small team of teachers from various disciplines.
- It recruits students who volunteer for the program and demonstrate their commitment through an application process.
- It focuses on a career theme in a field in which demand is growing and good employment opportunities exist in the local labor market. The curriculum combines technical and academic content, usually through one technical and

14

three academic classes each semester. Generic employability skills are also included. An academy keeps open students' option to attend college.

- Students are employed during the summer and (in some academies) part time during the school year in jobs related to their field of study.
- Employer representatives from the academy career field help plan and guide the program and are involved as speakers, field trip hosts, job supervisors, and sometimes mentors for individual students.
- Classes that are smaller than is typical in the high school, a system of motivational activities and rewards, and regular contacts with parents contribute to students' sense of membership in a caring community.
- A mixture of outside funding (in California through state grants), district backing, and employer contributions supports the program. Academies usually increase the cost of educating students somewhat, primarily through increased teacher costs and private sector involvement.

While most academies share all these characteristics, some place more emphasis on technical training, others on academics. The student target group also varies. Originally the Philadelphia Academies focused on dropout prevention; over time this has changed, however, and a broader cross section of students can now enroll. Academies sponsored by the National Academy Foundation (NAF) combine academic and occupational studies for a cross section of youth, college-bound or otherwise, who wish to explore a career area. NAF policy requires sex equity and a racial mix reflecting the student population of the host high school.

The California Partnership Academies emphasize both academics and technical training. They have focused primarily on at-risk students, although here, too, the target group is beginning to broaden. This book will focus primarily on the California Partnership Academies, in part because our experience happens to have been in California, and in part because the California model is the only one so far that has been defined by legislation (see the Appendix).

Specific goals of the California Partnership Academies are to

- Improve school performance and graduation rates of at-risk students
- Raise students' ambitions and career options beyond those of the regular high school program
- Provide an academic foundation and technical skills that will enable students to continue their education beyond high school, obtain employment leading to desirable careers, or both
- Satisfy local demand for skilled employees in the academy's occupational field

Structure Within a High School

Students enrolled in a California Partnership Academy take three academic classes and one technical class in the academy each semester during grades 10 and 11. The academic classes are usually English, math, and science or social studies. The technical class depends on the occupational theme of the academy. The set of academy classes is often reduced to just the technical class and perhaps one or two academic classes in grade 12. Each of these classes is restricted to academy participants.

All other required and elective courses are taken in regular classes along with nonacademy students at the high school. All courses in the academy meet high school graduation requirements and contribute to a diploma. Academy students must earn a regular high school diploma. They are encouraged to go on for additional education beyond high school, and most do, usually starting in a community college. Table 2.1 presents the three-year sequence of courses and related activities in a California Partnership Academy.

Table 2.1. California Partnership Academy
Three-Year Progression of Courses and Activities.

Grade 10	Grade 11	Summer	Grade 12
Students enter program	Classes: English, math, science or social studies, technical	Summer school if needed	Classes: Technical, perhaps English and/
Classes: English, math, science or social studies, technical		Summer jobs in a local company provided for students who are performing well	or economics; mainstreamed in other classes
Elective classes	Elective classes		Preparation for
Speakers and field trips	Speakers and field trips	Close supervision	either college entry or work
Motivational activities	Motivational activities	End-of-summer rating	Possible after-noon part-time work
Parental support	Mentor program		

Part of the program structure involves block scheduling of academy classes. Usually this means scheduling the four academy classes during the first four periods of the morning. This leaves the remaining periods for other required and elective courses. Scheduling the four classes together allows the program to arrange activities for all classes at the same time—for example, listening to speakers from the business community or going on field trips. It also allows for team teaching when two or three teachers want to work together on a lesson or project.

Some academies also offer preacademy programs. For example, NAF offers a program for preacademy students that includes a course entitled "Strategies for Success." This course is designed to enhance students' reading, listening, and studying skills, as well as their self-esteem.

Curriculum

A career academy curriculum combines academic and technical content. Both are essential, and the two are integrated, showing the relationship between academic skills and real-world jobs. The field of technical training is selected through an analysis of the local labor market to determine which field offers the best employment possibilities and will lead to substantial employer support.

As of the 1991–92 school year, there were more than twenty career fields on which academies had chosen to focus. California alone had developed programs in seventeen different fields:

- Agribusiness
- Business applications of computers
- Communication and video technology
- Construction
- Education
- Electronics
- Finance
- Health and health science
- Hospital and hotels
- Internal Revenue Service administration
- International trade and business
- Law and government
- Media and graphic arts
- Natural resources and environmental technology
- Retail trade and marketing
- Space
- Transportation

In addition, Philadelphia has academies focused in several fields, including electrical, business, applied automotive and mechanical sciences, and health. By early 1992 the National Academy Foundation had established or planned academies of finance in twenty-four cities around the country and academies of travel and tourism in eleven cities. Washington, D.C., has begun an NAF academy in public service and is planning others in transportation, leadership, and health and human services, all associated with departments of the federal government. Many other themes are possible.

Simply identifying a strong occupational theme is not sufficient, however. Coordination between academic and vocational instruction is an essential part of the academy curriculum. As discussed in Chapter One, traditionally these two categories of instruction have been taught separately. Not only have teachers from the two realms had little contact but there has been a class distinction between them. Vocational education has been seen as a place where lower-performing students not heading for college are tracked.

However, the methods of vocational education, which include much "learning by doing" and applied instruction, are now seen by some learning theorists as a superior way to teach all subjects including those that are abstract and theoretical (Raizen, 1989; Resnick, 1987b). To improve education for all students, including the college-bound, it is helpful to apply principles traditionally embodied in vocational education: introducing material in practical contexts and showing the relationship between academic disciplines and various careers. Even those planning to attend four-year colleges can benefit since they, too, are work-bound eventually and most of them will be employed while they attend college.

Academies integrate academic and vocational instruction. The very structure of the program encourages this through the close alliance between the technical teacher and the academic ones in planning the program. They have a common planning period each day in which to meet and coordinate their efforts. Students' employment in jobs related to their fields of study, and their other contacts with employers in the field, also help put their academic work into a practical context.

Integrating the curriculum means coordinating courses so that a given topic is analyzed from different angles in more than one course. Here are two illustrations from the California Partnership Academies.

1. The electronics academy at Sequoia High School in Redwood City has developed integrated curricula around its electronics theme. Several classes take up related topics at the same time:

    Electronics: direct current circuits
    Science: batteries, making electric motors
    Math: Ohm's Law, measuring work, electricity
    English: writing a paper on how to construct a capacitor

2. The health academy at Blair High School in Pasadena has developed a unit around the book *The Andromeda Strain.* Topics in different classes are related:

> English: the literary features of the book, such as plot, character, and theme
> Health: effects and treatment of viruses
> Science: how cells and immune systems operate
> Math: the geometric progression of unchecked viruses

By using career-related examples to illustrate lessons, academies bring subjects alive and encourage the use of thinking skills. Assessment is done not just through class tests but also through students' application of knowledge to laboratory exercises taught in the technical classes, and ultimately to their jobs. Employers' ratings of students' job performance are carefully studied and fed back to students. For most students, and especially for those unmotivated by traditional academic curricula and methodology, this real-life learning makes education more meaningful.

In addition to the integration between occupational fields and academic subjects, academies also infuse into their curricula lessons about work ethics and behavior, sometimes called "employability skills." Topics covered in these lessons include

- Researching companies and jobs in the field
- Analyzing one's own job skills and interests
- Developing résumés
- Completing job applications
- Undergoing job interviews
- Dressing and behaving appropriately on the job

Students are introduced to the expectations of the workplace concerning dress, language, and behavior. They are taught that they must work well with others and be responsible, dependable, and punctual. They are encouraged to view themselves as representatives of their schools, communities, and fellow academy students. The experience of applying for and obtaining a summer job at the end of the junior year and a part-time afternoon job during the senior year reinforces these lessons.

The combination of the school-within-a-school structure and integrated academic-vocational curricula respond to several of the issues discussed in Chapter One. The rigor of academics is brought to all subjects, as is the relevance of vocational training. Students learn by doing and apply their knowledge of academic subjects to solving work-related tasks and problems. The curriculum has a clear focus and points students toward a postgraduate goal around which they can organize their high school learning. This enhances motivation for students whether or not they plan to attend college.

Staffing and Management

Management of the program is usually shared between a school district administrator and the teachers in the program. Districts containing more than one NAF academy usually have a full-time director. Where there is an active district administrator, he or she is usually responsible for

- Initial program planning
- Start-up of the program
- Development and integration of the curriculum
- Coordination with local employers
- Program evaluation
- Reports to the superintendent and school board

The core teaching staff usually consists of four teachers, three academic (English, math, and science or social studies) and one technical (in the career theme field). Like the students, they are members by choice: the district administrator informs the general staff at the high school about the program, and those who are interested apply. To be successful, teachers must be willing to work with the type of student the program seeks out, take on a variety of extra program responsibilities, and coordinate their activities with involved employers.

During the first year, when there are only sophomores in the program, these teachers each have two academy sections in their respective field. During the second year and beyond they have two sections added at grade 11, for a total of four. This means they are involved at successive grade levels with the same set of students and thus are able not only to coordinate the curriculum across the two years but also to see the student development that takes place. Many teachers comment on the satisfaction this brings.

Where districts can afford it, academy teachers are accorded an extra preparation period for their additional responsibilities. Since the usual teaching load is five classes with one preparation period, this four-period assignment, with the extra common planning period, becomes their full load. Teachers invariably cite this planning period as an important contribution to the success of the program. They use the time to provide individualized attention to students, contact parents, hold staff meetings to discuss student problems, plan curriculum integration, and plan incentive award ceremonies and other program activities.

Usually one of the four teachers takes on the role of "lead teacher" of the program. This person must have at least one extra preparation period and is often provided two. He or she has a number of coordinating responsibilities:

- Chairing (or cochairing) steering committee meetings
- Chairing teacher staff meetings
- Orienting new teachers
- Managing staff development
- Handling supplies and the budget
- Coordinating with the district and high school administration
- Arranging room allocations and class schedules

The lead teacher can be from any discipline, depending on who wants to take on these responsibilities.

An important feature of an academy is that all the teachers who work in it have a greater role in planning the program and making decisions about it than is the case in most schools. They play a role in the program's many components: developing the curriculum, organizing the school-within-a-school structure, selecting students, coordinating the curricular integration and related activities in their classes, and managing involvement of the business community. Teachers in most academies have two reactions to being in the program: they find it harder work than their previous teaching assignments, and they like it better because of the sense of ownership they have and their closer connections to students, which last over a three-year period.

Parents also play an important supporting role. One teacher is usually given the responsibility for maintaining contact with them through phone calls, a program newsletter, and face-to-face meetings when there are problems. Parents are expected to attend a back-to-school night in the fall and special awards functions such as the year-end graduation ceremony. They are also expected to reinforce with their children the need to take the program seriously and keep up with assignments. While it is often difficult for busy parents to play an active role in program activities, turnouts at program events are usually much higher than for non-academy classes and sometimes astonish school officials. Academy experience suggests that parents respond positively when they are actively involved in the decision to enroll their children in a program and are asked to follow through on that commitment.

Target Group and Student Selection

Who is eligible to participate in a career academy? As mentioned earlier, there are variations from one program to another. California Partnership Academies have targeted at-risk students thought to be in danger of dropping out of high school before graduation. Indicators of risk include patterns of irregular attendance, low grades, fewer than needed credits, and economic disadvantages. Often low-socioeconomic or minority status correlates with these, as does limited English proficiency. Some of these students are confronting serious personal problems, such as pregnancy, dysfunctional families, or drug abuse.

An evaluation conducted in California provides a profile of the students enrolled in the California Partnership Academies during the 1987–88 school year (Dayton, Weisberg, and Stern, 1989). In that year, 52 percent of the program's members statewide were male and 48 percent were female. Five percent were Asian/Pacific Islander, 26 percent black, 29 percent Hispanic, 36 percent white, and 3 percent other. By comparison, the percentages for the state generally in grades K through 12 during 1986–87 (the nearest comparable data) were 8 percent Asian/Pacific Islander, 9 percent black, 30 percent Hispanic, 51 percent white, and 2 percent other (Guthrie and others, 1988). Minority enrollment is larger at the lower grades, so this slightly overstates the general high school minority rates in 1986–87. The academies evidently enrolled relatively large proportions of African Americans and Hispanics.

In both Philadelphia and California the academy model is being used increasingly with a broader cross section of students defined primarily by their interest in the selected field of training. This is also the policy for NAF academies. This policy avoids the stigma often associated with a program limited to disadvantaged students. It puts the program in a better position to reduce class and race divisions. It provides stronger student role models for at-risk members of the program to emulate. It increases the interest of many employers in supporting the program and hiring its graduates. As a model for high school reform and restructuring, this approach offers far broader applications.

An important feature of academies is that students enroll in them by choice. They are not just assigned to the program, as is often the case in other high school programs. Students are presented with information about the academy during the spring semester of their pre-academy year, and those who are interested must take the initiative to apply. In many academies there is more demand for the program than there are positions available. In some instances, as many as five hundred students have applied for fifty positions in an academy.

Selection of students for a California Partnership Academy usually proceeds by a sequence such as the following:

1. Information about the program is disseminated by means of class visits to ninth graders thought likely to be interested. Also, referrals are sought from teachers and counselors.
2. A group meeting, usually one period in length, provides more detailed information. Interested students are asked to complete an application.
3. Information about those who have applied is collected to determine whether they are appropriate candidates. This is particularly the case when the academy is directed toward at-risk students. The data include past attendance, grades, credits, test scores, and teacher and counselor opinions.
4. Academy staff hold interviews with applicants who are appropriate candidates, either individually or in small groups.
5. A parent meeting is held, usually in the evening, for both parents and students, to ensure that the student's interest in the program is supported by the family and to enlist the parents' support for the three-year commitment involved.
6. Based on all of the above steps, a final selection is made.

All of this occurs during the spring semester of the students' ninth-grade year. In most schools, the process begins in late February or March and is completed sometime in May, to allow time for the students to be fit into the fall class schedule. In a California Partnership Academy, forty to fifty students are selected each year. They are divided into two sections for each of the four academy classes, so that class size is twenty to twenty-five.

In NAF academies the selection procedure is similar to the sequence of steps listed above. However, the NAF procedure does not include the collection of information described in step 3. In addition, NAF students and parents must sign a memorandum of understanding. Some NAF academies also offer pre-academy programs that let younger students explore the academy theme.

Employer Involvement

The partnership between schools and local employers is central to a career academy. Employers play several essential roles, including

- Serving on a steering committee that guides program development and establishes policies and procedures
- Volunteering as speakers to help motivate students and teach them about the field selected and the jobs they can aim for
- Hosting field trips to places of business, to show students what workplaces and jobs are like in practice
- Acting as mentors—forming one-to-one relationships as career-related big brothers and sisters
- Providing paid jobs for juniors and seniors proceeding toward on-time graduation

Early in the planning of an academy it is necessary to establish a committee that will guide the program. This usually includes representatives from several employers as well as one or more of the academy teachers (especially the lead teacher) and a school and/or district administrator. Often called a steering committee, this body usually oversees a number of task forces or subcommittees working on such topics as curriculum development, speakers and field trips, the mentor and work experience programs, and resource identification and supply. It sets policies for the program and ensures that the views of both business and education are incorporated in its management.

It is important early in the program to begin to give students examples of successful role models from the academy's occupational field. For this reason academies usually have an active speaker program during the sophomore year, and perhaps during the junior year as well, with speakers every few weeks. The speakers inform students about the advantages and disadvantages of various jobs that exist in the field, so that students can begin to develop their own career plans. Speakers also give students a sense of what education and training are necessary for various jobs.

Field trips are more complicated and expensive than speakers, but they expose students to the actual job conditions under which people in various companies and jobs work. If hosted and led by someone knowledgeable, they give students information about jobs and training in the field as well as at the particular company being visited. Academies usually conduct four or more field trips per year, especially during the sophomore year.

The mentor program generally operates primarily during the junior year. It is designed to give each student an individual contact through whom he or she can gain more information about jobs in the field and about the many details of being a successful employee. Mentors are asked to devote at least two hours per month to the program. Activities range from giving the student a tour of the mentor's workplace and introducing him or her to co-workers to visiting the student at the high school to see his or her "place of work," attending job fairs or technical shows, and having the student shadow the mentor at work.

The broadening exposure provided by speakers, field trips, and mentors, combined with the academic and technical training the students receive in their classes, culminates with a paid job during the summer following the junior year, which often continues during the afternoons of the senior year. Most students approach this event with a certain degree of trepidation. They must complete job applications, undergo interviews, and await decisions about their hiring. They are not guaranteed a job, only an interview. Some must go through several interviews before they are hired, and a few may prove unready.

The fact that most academies have been able to involve employers in most of these components of the program indicates that business representatives find the activities appropriate and satisfying. Many employers in fact comment that they like the clear definition of their roles provided by an academy, rather than the more usual approach of schools to companies that is amorphous and ad hoc in nature. They also like the outcome-based orientation of the program, with its focused curriculum and performance-based funding. Estimates provided during the 1990–91 school year suggest that the average California academy garnered over $80,000 in employer support. Most of this was in the form of personnel involvement. Academies provide a vehicle for employers to share in the responsibility of preparing young people for their careers.

Enrichment and Motivational Features

A description of the formal components of the academy model leaves out one feature that is critical. This is the central role of motivational activities and reward structures. Since at least in the dropout prevention version of the model the participants are students who are not excelling in school, it is important to provide as many incentives as possible to increase their motivation. This is accomplished in several ways.

Perhaps the most important motivating feature of academies is their family-like atmosphere. The school-within-a-school structure and smaller classes let students stay with the same classmates through four classes each day, so that they become a cohesive group. The fact that the teachers work closely with one another enhances this effect. Teachers get to know their students well, a process that builds over the course of three years.

Special activities are also designed to motivate students. There are many awards, such as for best attendance, best math or English student of the month, or most innovative technical project. Teachers hold awards luncheons, inviting parents and mentors. They give out plaques, certificates, and other rewards. At the end of the year a graduation ceremony features a distinguished speaker and many awards. All of this contributes to the students' sense of success and their self-esteem, helping them build the confidence necessary to complete high school and enter a challenging field of work.

Financial Support

Academies vary in how much additional funding they receive, and from where. They almost always need some additional support over and above the basic average daily attendance (ADA) funding determined in state formulas. Usually this support comes from some combination of district and private sector sources.

In California the state provides a limited number of grants to districts; these are awarded through competitions held each year. Once such a grant is won, it continues indefinitely; it is not just for start-up. However, it must be matched with in-kind contributions from both the receiving school district and supporting companies. The maximum amount of the grant in 1991–92 was $67,500. This may be increased somewhat within the next year or two.

Districts receiving California Partnership Academy grants usually meet the required match largely by providing academy teachers with an extra preparation period (a one-period reduction in their teaching load) and with class sizes of no more than twenty-five students (the average in California is around thirty). Together these typically cost a district an amount equal to one or two full-time teachers. Businesses meet the match primarily by donating personnel time to engage in all the activities described earlier in this chapter (acting as steering committee members, speakers, field trip hosts, mentors, and work experience supervisors). They may also contribute equipment (for example, computers) and supplies.

The precise amount of the state grant in California is determined by the number of students enrolled in the academy who are performing adequately. Programs are reimbursed only for students who have at least 80 percent daily attendance and earn 90 percent of the credits required for "normal progress toward graduation" for the year. A first-year academy must qualify thirty students to obtain the maximum grant, a second-year academy sixty students, and a third-year academy (and beyond) ninety students. Given typical attrition, enrolling forty to fifty students in each new sophomore class usually results in a full three-year program with about one hundred students.

There are many costs associated with an academy. One of these is facilities. Another is the expense of coordinating employers' involvement and students' work experience. Transportation is required for field trips and other program activities. Books and supplies are needed. Awards may cost money.

The state grant is insufficient by itself to cover personnel and other costs. This is the reason for the matches required of the district and supporting employers. Districts vary in their contribution, but the more successful academies usually enjoy strong district support. In California the total additional revenue from all sources typically amounts to $750 to $1,000 per student per year once the program is fully operational (Stern, Dayton, Paik, and Weisberg, 1989). Given the approximately $4,500-per-year average allotment for high school students in the state, this represents an addition of roughly 20 percent above base revenues for operating a program that incorporates all the features of the California Partnership Academy model. The cost could be reduced by eliminating some of these features.

Importance of a Model

This presentation of the career academy model should serve the immediate purpose of explaining what this book is about. It should also help clarify how career academies address fundamental problems of high schools by linking them to the world outside, placing academic course material in a practical context, and combining relevance with rigor in order to avoid creating a second-class program. Some of this will be further explained in subsequent chapters.

Chapter Three describes how the current career academies have come into being. This is where a model has importance in practice. As the chapter recounts, models have been used as templates or blueprints for creating networks of mutually supporting career academy programs.

THREE

⊶ ○ ⊷

Evolution of
the Academy Movement

Although earlier precursors can be found, the current academy movement has been a continuous progression from the founding of the first Philadelphia Academy in 1969. After several replications in Philadelphia, in 1981 the model was transplanted to California, where two programs began on the San Francisco Peninsula. Documented success of the Peninsula Academies prompted the California legislature to establish partnership academies throughout the state. Meanwhile, in an independent development, the American Express Company in 1982 began an academy of finance in New York City. This, too, was replicated, and in 1989 the National Academy Foundation (NAF) was formed to promote academies of finance, academies of travel and tourism, and other academies nationwide. This chapter tells how these events unfolded.

In addition to chronicling some of these events for the first time, this chapter may provide some insights into the process of educational change. A well-known paradox of public education in the United States is that highly decentralized governance has produced very similar practices and problems everywhere. Teachers have wide latitude to choose their own methods, school sites can design their own programs, district school boards can adopt their own policies, and individual states can write their own laws. Yet the problems of high schools described in the first chapter—fragmented subject matter disconnected from the world outside, fifty-minute periods, chalk-and-talk instruction, apathetic students—are ubiquitous. The fact that teachers, school sites, districts, and states have much control implies that any new solutions must be locally acceptable and adaptable. But the fact that common culture and basic institutional forces have produced similar results in different places also suggests that new solutions applied in one location may work in others as well. Effective educational change would seem to require a model that recognizes institutional and cultural constraints, and a network that communicates the model from one place to another, giving outside legitimacy to new ideas while at the same time leaving implementation in the hands of local authorities. This is, in fact, how the career academy model has spread.

The Philadelphia, California, and NAF academies discussed in this chapter all share most elements of the career academy model described in Chapter Two. Another existing set of programs, sponsored by the Burger King Corporation and Cities in Schools, Inc., also call themselves academies. They are designed to provide individualized instruction, counseling, and employment assistance to students who have already dropped out of school or are in danger of dropping out. However, the Burger King academies differ from career academies. They do not attempt to organize a whole curriculum around a career theme or to prepare students for college as well as for work. While they appear to provide valuable services for some students, the Burger King academies in their present form are not sufficiently comprehensive to serve as a model for reforming the entire high school, and they will not be discussed here.

Philadelphia: A Network in One School District

The current wave of vocational academies began in Philadelphia in 1969 with the opening of the electrical academy at Thomas Edison High School (Neubauer, 1986; Snyder and

McMullan, 1987a). At the time, Edison had the highest drop-out rate and lowest attendance rate in the city. The academy was to keep students in school and prepare them for employment. The Philadelphia Urban Coalition initiated the idea and coordinated the planning.

The electrical academy was considered successful enough to warrant replication. In 1972 the Philadelphia business academy opened at University City High School, and in 1975 a second business academy began at South Philadelphia High School. An academy of applied automotive and mechanical sciences started at Simon Gratz High School in 1974. An umbrella organization, the Philadelphia High School Academy Association (PHSAA), was created to support these efforts and maintain communication between city business leaders and top school district officials.

From 1970 through October 1988, each individual academy and the PHSAA were separately incorporated, non-profit, tax-exempt organizations. Each academy had its own board of directors, which, along with the association's board, managed its individual programs. However, by 1986 two studies of the academies' administrative structures had concluded that, in order to accomplish the desired expansion of their programs, the academies should consolidate into one organization. Accordingly, in November 1988 the individual academies merged with the PHSAA, which was later renamed the Philadelphia High School Academies, Inc. (PHSA).

The board of directors of PHSA includes leaders from business, labor, and the school district, as do the boards of governors of the individual academy programs. The PHSA board, which includes chief executives of area corporations as well as the superintendent of schools, is responsible for overall policy, fundraising, and budget approval. Each academy's board of governors is responsible for overseeing its program's budget, giving approval for its academy's expansion to new schools, and maintaining relations with the local private sector.

More than 90 percent of the PHSA budget comes from the private sector and foundations. Local businesses gave

$400,000 in cash or in kind to Philadelphia Academies in 1987–88 and $830,000 in 1988–89 (Hinds, 1990).

The Philadelphia Academies expanded further in the 1980s. A health academy opened in 1982 at Martin Luther King, Jr., High School. By 1986 the business academy was operating in five high schools and the other academies had expanded to a total of five other high schools. As of 1991 eight different academy programs were operating in sixteen Philadelphia high schools. Business academies were running in nine schools; health academies in four schools; hotel, restaurant and tourism academies in three schools; academies of automotive technology in two schools; and electrical academies in two schools. Academies of environmental technology and horticulture and an academy for fitness, health promotion, and sports education were each operating in one high school. Six high schools (Lincoln, South Philadelphia, West Philadelphia, Franklin, Washington, and Frankford) housed academies in more than one career area (Philadelphia High School Academies, 1991).

In June 1991 the Philadelphia Academies enrolled 2,024 students in grades 9 through 12. These included 1,372 African American students, 128 Hispanic students, and 49 Asian students. Projected enrollment in September 1991 was approximately twenty-seven hundred—more than triple the number of students in Philadelphia Academies in June 1985. The goal is to enroll five thousand of Philadelphia's public comprehensive high school students in academy programs (Philadelphia High School Academies, 1991).

New Emphasis on Preparation for College

The original Philadelphia Academies were designed to prepare students for occupations not ordinarily requiring a bachelor's degree: electrical trades, secretarial work, automotive mechanics. These programs fit within the traditional limits of high school vocational education as defined by the federal Smith-Hughes Act of 1917 (U.S. Congress, 1917). What distinguished the Philadelphia Academies was the school-within-a-school format, which was designed to build more social cohesion among students, and which also demanded that academic and vocational teachers coordinate their curricula. Philadelphia Academies "link the development of basic reading, computing, and communication skills to the development of technical and attitudinal skills. . . . The direct relationship of math and English to job skills—be they electrical, mechanical, or other—motivates students to learn and helps them see the importance of their learning." Provision of related employment during the summer and part-time during the year further enhances students' motivation: "Academic skills are linked to the vocational curriculum, and the vocational curriculum is linked to a paycheck" (Philadelphia High School Academies, 1991).

During the 1980s, however, the Philadelphia health academy took off in a somewhat different direction. Instead of focusing on placement of students in full-time jobs after graduation, the health academy transcended the traditional limits of high school vocational education by emphasizing preparation for college. The curriculum requires four years of math, science, and foreign language—including a semester of Latin to give students a basis for understanding medical and pharmacological terminology. As the health academy's executive director put it in 1986, "the other academies infused a vocational training program with academics. In the health academy, we infused an academic curriculum with a vocational orientation" (Snyder and McMullan, 1987a, p. D-29). A 1991 survey of health academy graduates from Overbrook and Martin Luther King High Schools found that 75 percent of the graduating class of 1989 and 85 percent of the class of 1990 were attending college. About half of those attending college said they planned careers in health care or medicine (Philadelphia High School Academies, 1991, p. 3).

The Peninsula Academies

In 1981 the Philadelphia Academy model was transplanted to the Sequoia Union High School District on the peninsula south of San Francisco, California. The Sequoia district lies just north of Silicon Valley, renowned for its electronics industry. Four comprehensive high schools, grades 9 through 12, serve sixty-five hundred students from eight small cities. The social composition ranges from highly educated, affluent, and white to educationally disadvantaged, poor, and minority (primarily Hispanic and African American). Students are bused from the minority communities to each of the high schools to achieve racial balance.

In the late 1970s the Sequoia school district began to experience rapid growth in its percentage of minority, limited-English-proficient, and other educationally disadvantaged students. At the same time, many other students were confronting major personal problems, such as drug abuse and dysfunctional families, which were causing them to become alienated from and indifferent toward high school. A significant number of these students had little motivation to succeed and were dropping out of school unprepared for work. And those who managed to graduate were found to lack the skills required for entry-level positions in local companies. At a time when overall unemployment was under 5 percent, unemployment among minorities was approaching 20 percent—50 percent among minority youth.

In 1980 Hattie Harlow, director of the Mid-Peninsula Urban Coalition, a local community-based organization involved in improving minority employment, brought the Philadelphia Academies program to the attention of Harry Reynolds, then superintendent of the Sequoia district. Reynolds decided to create the Peninsula Academies program in two schools: the computer academy at Menlo-Atherton High School and the electronics academy at Sequoia High School. The school district lacked the financial and technical resources required to develop the program, so Reynolds asked the coalition to act as a broker to help obtain the required funding and other necessary resources through a business partnership and foundation grants.

During the initial phase of the program the Mid-Peninsula Urban Coalition took the lead in directing the program and bringing together the business and school partners. It also took on some responsibility for student recruitment and total responsibility for job placement and for liaison between the job sites and the school personnel. After the third year the coalition's management role was gradually phased out as the academies program became a bilateral partnership between business and the school district.

Division of Labor

Two committees composed of representatives from the Mid-Peninsula Urban Coalition, the school district, and business were formed to do the early planning and determine the curriculum required. One of these, the "executive committee," involved top-level managers and focused on resource development. The other, the "steering committee," involved staff members and dealt with implementation issues such as curriculum development, student selection, and classroom preparation. Eventually the two merged into one.

The executive committee was charged with securing active business participation in the program. The committee found that to involve business successfully three objectives must be met: (1) companies must take specific responsibilities and roles that are important to the success of the program, (2) they must expect to sustain their commitment over time, and (3) a sufficient number of companies must agree to share the major responsibilities and provide resources. An initial group of companies promised to provide jobs, mentors, speakers, and field trip sites. They also agreed to promote the program and help gain the involvement of other firms.

The steering committee formed several task forces. The curriculum task force began its work by determining the technical skills needed by business. This preliminary curriculum work was important to the success of the program, but it was only a beginning. Marilyn Raby, the Sequoia district administrator responsible for the academies, decided to make the program as academically rigorous as possible, in contrast to the traditional vocational education approach of a training program with some academic skills attached. Although she met with some initial resistance, Raby was convinced that no one could possibly predict what types of jobs the students would ultimately have; therefore, a solid academic foundation was required if they were to be prepared for future work.

Other task forces dealt with additional matters. The school operations task force oversaw day-to-day operation of the program, such as scheduling and setting performance standards. The student task force handled student recruitment and selection strategies. The resources task force, at the direction of the executive committee, arranged for business participation in the form of mentors, guest speakers, and field trip sites. The curriculum development task force ensured that the curriculum met the needs of business, represented current and emerging practices, met state curriculum and vocational education standards, and complied with Sequoia district graduation requirements. The work experience task force obtained mentor and work experience positions from business, starting in the program's second year.

Recruiting Teachers

The academies' teaching staff was recruited in the spring of 1981. The superintendent and members of his staff made presentations at each school to ask for volunteers. Only three teachers in a school district of over three hundred teachers volunteered. The other teachers required were hired specifically for the program. The vocational/technical courses in computers and electronics were taught by personnel on loan from two participating companies, Lockheed Missiles and Space Corporation and Hewlett-Packard.

The reluctance of the district's existing teaching staff to participate may have reflected their perception that the academies were just another vocational education/work experience program. Teacher union members did not want extra funds expended on the academies for fear of cutting into the regular program and salary increases. Others were concerned that their participation might arouse their colleagues' envy because of the academies' smaller class sizes, instructional sides, and released planning period. In addition, there was reluctance to take on classes composed exclusively of at-risk youth. This concern was compounded by the fact that the students entered the program with a broad range of abilities, skills, and attitudes. Classes composed of such students are more difficult to teach than regular classes.

The concerns of the teaching staff were resolved over time as a result of the academies staff making a concerted effort to win over their colleagues by making them aware of the academies teachers' extra responsibilities and the otherwise unavailable opportunities provided for the targeted youth. School site administrators helped explain and support the academies concept by making presentations at faculty and department meetings. Academies shared their employer contacts with staff from work experience and other vocational education programs, thus minimizing competition for students, jobs, and program prestige.

Awards and Recognition

Over the course of the next several years, the Peninsula Academies won a number of awards. The National Academy for Vocational Education in 1985 named them an exemplary program. The academies received a Private Sector Initiative commendation from the president of the United States in 1986, a Distinguished Performance Award from the National Alliance of Business in 1987, and extensive local and national media coverage ranging from articles in The *New York Times* and the *Phi Delta Kappan* to a PBS documentary on dropout prevention programs. The U.S. General Accounting Office (1987) included the Peninsula Academies among a set of featured dropout prevention programs.

In 1989 the U.S. Department of Education funded the business technology academies at the Sequoia district's other two high schools to serve as national demonstration sites for dropout prevention through the use of vocational education. These new academies are modeled on the Peninsula Academies. They focus on business technology and place major emphasis on the use of computer technology as a teaching/learning tool to accelerate student mastery of basic skills, critical thinking, and problem solving.

California Partnership Academies:
A Network in One State

By the third year of the Peninsula Academies there was evidence that the experiment was becoming a success. Students were remaining in the program, and their enthusiasm was generally high. The two high schools had come to accept the academies as ongoing parts of their programs. The first mentor program had been on balance a positive experience. The first summer jobs program had worked quite well, and the employed students returned in the fall brimming with self-confidence, based in part on very positive employer ratings of their work. The evaluation data showed clear differences between the academy students and their matched comparison group counterparts on measures such as retention, credits earned, and pass rates on the Sequoia district's proficiency tests. At the end of the third year the California School Board Association conferred its "Golden Bell" award on the program.

AB 3104: The First State Bill

It was at this time that the notion of replicating the academies began to surface. Few other programs serving at-risk students could show objective evidence of effectiveness. In the fall of 1983 the executive director of the Stanford Urban Coalition, Sarita Berry, and the coalition's academy director, Charles Dayton, arranged a meeting with the state assemblyman who represented the peninsula region, Byron Sher.

Much to their surprise, Assemblyman Sher not only failed to discourage their idea but felt that replicating academies in California was a genuinely worthwhile concept. He encouraged them to draft language that could be used in putting together a bill for this purpose. Dayton met with Sequoia district administrator Marilyn Raby, and together they worked on such language. This was submitted to Assemblyman Sher's office, and what resulted was the first academy replication bill, AB 3104. It was carried by Sher, a Democrat, on the Assembly side, and a high-ranking Republican, Robert Naylor, on the Senate side. The bill cleared all hurdles, and Governor George Deukmejian signed it on September 29, 1984.

The bill was very simple in its wording and approach. Beginning in January 1985 it would offer $25,000 planning grants to ten school districts, selected on a grants competition basis, to plan an academy from January through June; these would begin operation in the fall of 1985. Each site that successfully completed the planning process would then receive a $50,000 grant to implement its academy each year.

Each district that received a grant was required to match it with an equal amount of "direct and in-kind support provided by the district" and "direct and in-kind support provided by participating companies or a combination of participating companies and a business-related, community-based organization." The intent was to develop three-way partnerships among the state, school district, and supporting local companies.

The Peninsula Academies, after some initial financial difficulties, had been quite successful in raising foundation support for their efforts, amounting to more than $50,000 per year. They had also benefited from the Stanford Urban Coalition's provision of staff to involve businesses in the program. Further, their location at the north end of the Silicon Valley had made both their technical focus on computers and electronics and the involvement of large, well-off companies relatively easy. No one knew how well the process of replicating the academy model would work without these conditions. While AB 3104 called for an evaluation of the new academies by the State Department of Education two years after the effective date of the bill, no funds were appropriated for this work.

Results of Replication Under AB 3104

With these limitations, efforts went forward. A grants competition was held and ten sites were selected; planning efforts in these sites were carried out, with some limited help by the State Department of Education in combination with leaders of the Peninsula Academies. In the fall of 1985 ten new academies began operations.

Because of their interest in academies as a model for wider use with at-risk students, the Edna McConnell Clark Foundation in New York City and the William and Flora Hewlett Foundation in Menlo Park, California, provided funds to Policy Analysis for California Education (PACE) at the University of California, Berkeley, to evaluate these ten new academies for three years, from the fall of 1985 through June 1988. Charles Dayton, now a policy analyst with PACE, agreed to direct these evaluations. David Stern, an economist interested in the link between education and work, agreed to supervise the data analysis.

The results of these first ten replications were mixed. Two sites dropped out after the second year, one because of poor management at the school, the other because of lack of district support. Two others dropped out after the third year, for these reasons plus lack of private sector support.

In contrast, several academies took hold and thrived, producing evidence of positive performance by academy students relative to comparison groups. Among these were two electronics academies begun in the East Side Union High School District in San Jose, the health academy begun at Oakland Technical High School in Oakland, and a computer academy begun at Hiram Johnson High School in Sacramento. What was clear from this first round of replications, however, was that the replication process had been uneven. Most sites that had followed the academy model carefully and implemented the programs well had had good results, but several sites had failed to carry out the program design.

SB 605: The Second State Bill

AB 3104 had a legislated life span of just three years; by the end of 1987 it was scheduled to sunset. Thus during the 1987 legislative session a new bill was introduced, SB 605. This bill was drafted largely by Ray Schneyer, a semiretired special assistant to the president of Lockheed Missiles and Space Corporation, who also served as a trustee for the Stanford Urban Coalition.

The new bill was carried by Robert Naylor's replacement, Senator Rebecca Morgan. Again it received support from a number of influential companies that had worked to support academies and had become advocates for the academies program. It, too, cleared all legislative hurdles, and it was signed by Governor Deukmejian in September 1987.

SB 605 changed some of the provisions of the original bill. First, it provided a basis for up to fifteen new replications of the academy each year for the next four years; actual implementation depended on yearly funding decisions. Second, it made the funding of academies performance-based. That is, the programs had to submit data on how well their students had performed on measures of attendance (80 percent required) and credits earned (90 percent of those necessary for "normal progress toward graduation" required) in order to be reimbursed through the grant. Reimbursement occurred after the school year was over, not before it began. Districts were allocated funds based on a formula that required thirty students to qualify for the maximum grant the first year, sixty the second year, and ninety the third year and thereafter.

Another change in the new bill included a smaller planning grant—$15,000. However, the maximum implementation grant was raised to $67,500 per year. Also, the academy model was more clearly spelled out, and sites were required to agree to follow it more carefully in order to receive grants. Finally, the name was changed from "Peninsula Academy" to "Partnership Academy," reflecting the growth of programs statewide, not just on the San Francisco Peninsula. A copy of the bill is contained in the Appendix.

Given the evaluation findings from the first three years and the uneven pattern of replications that had occurred, the need to provide clearer guidelines and better technical assistance to new sites in planning their academies was evident. While funds were not allocated for this in the new bill, again the William and Flora Hewlett Foundation took the lead in pursuing such support. Along with the Luke B. Hancock Foundation, based in nearby Palo Alto, it provided funds to the Stanford Urban Coalition to supply such technical assistance support.

Technical Assistance Network

A committee of veteran academy teachers, administrators, and private sector supporters was organized for this purpose. This "technical assistance group" began by encouraging a network of contacts among the dozen or so academies functioning at the time, and between them and the new ones identified for grants that year. It began to assemble materials that had been developed over the years describing components of the program, including student selection, mentors, and work experience. This was packaged in a three-hundred-page Resource Guide. The group also organized a statewide conference for the spring of 1989, with workshops focused on many academy components and operational tasks.

The technical assistance group continues to operate. It has developed additional materials, in particular a series of curricular guides for academies focusing on various occupational themes (computers, electronics, health), as well as examples of curricula, including lessons for teaching students how to find and keep jobs and lessons continuing academic and vocational subjects. Statewide conferences have been held each year, with 200 to 250 attendees.

Support by California Department of Education

In the fall of 1990 changes within the California Department of Education affected the Partnership Academies dramatically.

To foster academic-vocational integration, vocational education was moved from a division in which it was largely autonomous to the Curriculum and Instruction Division, where it came under the leadership of a new associate superintendent for high schools. Meanwhile, the outgoing state director of vocational education, James Allison, agreed to take on the role of state administrator for Partnership Academies.

With staff support, and with a high level of experience on which to draw, Allison provided the academies with a new degree of attention and management skill within the department. In addition, the emphasis that the new Carl D. Perkins Act (U.S. Congress, 1990) placed on academic-vocational integration and partnerships between schools and business, along with the California Department of Education's endorsement of these ideas, have given academies new importance as models for educational reform.

Superintendent of Public Instruction William Honig has become a strong advocate of the academies and offers them as a model for wider use in his presentations around the state. The deputy superintendent responsible for high schools and vocational education is also a strong supporter and encourages districts to use their Perkins Act funds to establish academies. In short, the California legislature, governor's office, and Department of Education have all contributed significantly to the development of academies in California.

National Academy Foundation: A Nationwide Network

Quite independent of developments in Philadelphia and California, events were unfolding in New York City that would later give birth to the National Academy Foundation (NAF).

Academy of Finance

The first academy of finance was started in 1982 as a pilot project between the American Express Company, the brokerage firm of Shearson Lehman Hutton (now Shearson Lehman Brothers), and the New York City public schools. (This and all other information pertaining to the academy of finance and the National Academy Foundation was obtained from NAF written materials supplemented by interviews with Phyllis Frankfort, executive director of the NAF.) Sandy Weill, then chairman of Shearson/American Express, was frustrated by the growing number of entry-level positions in the financial services field that could not be filled by the graduates of New York City high schools. He joined forces with the New York City Board of Education to support the development of a program that would improve students' preparation for work. Phyllis Frankfort, an administrator with the board of education and member of the mayor's task force to restructure occupational education, was selected to spearhead the joint effort. Her mission was to design and implement a high school finance curriculum that was academic but also career oriented.

Frankfort chose John Dewey High School in Brooklyn as the site for the first academy of finance. It began in February 1983 with thirty-five students. The curriculum was developed and teachers trained as the semester progressed. By the following fall, the program was serving two hundred students in five New York City schools. In September 1985 academies of finance opened in Minneapolis, Phoenix, and Broward County, Florida. The first annual student conference was held that year, as was the first institute for staff development. As of 1991 the academy of finance program had spread to fifty public high schools in twenty-two cities around the country. It had been validated by the U.S. Department of Education's National Diffusion Network, permitting NAF to obtain federal funds to support further expansion.

The academy of finance is a two- to four-year comprehensive program for high school students, designed to connect the classroom and the workplace. In addition to required academic courses, the curriculum includes two or three specialized finance courses, such as The World of Finance, College Accounting, Security Operations, Banking and Credit, Financial Products and Planning, and International Finance.

Students are required to take at least one related course in a local college. Some schools also offer pre-academy programs for freshmen or sophomores.

In addition to such course material, students gain direct exposure to work in the financial sector. After their junior year, students in good standing are eligible to apply for paid summer internships in local financial service companies. Students also take field trips to financial firms, attend conferences, and meet business leaders.

Other Academies

Encouraged by its success with the academy of finance, in 1986 American Express began a new program, the academy of travel and tourism, in New York City and Miami. As of 1991 nineteen academies of travel and tourism were planned or operating in fourteen cities. Like the academy of finance, the academy of travel and tourism is a two- to four-year comprehensive program that includes an academic core plus specialized courses, such as Introduction to Travel and Tourism, Destination Geography, Tourism Computer Applications, Travel as a Business, Economics for Travel and Tourism, and Writing/Research for Travel and Tourism. Students also have a range of personal contacts with employers in the field, and they are eligible for paid summer internships after their junior year. The National Academy Foundation makes available to any school a three-week module for grades 7 and 8 to increase students' awareness of the travel and tourism industry.

National Academy Foundation

In 1987 Phyllis Frankfort proposed the creation of a national office to provide coordination and quality control. In 1989 American Express and others formed NAF (Schmidt, 1989). Chairman of the board of directors was Vernon Jordan, Jr., a prominent civil rights leader, former president of the National Urban League, and also a member of the board of directors of the American Express Company. The president of NAF's board was William Brock, who served as U.S. trade representative and then secretary of labor in the Reagan administration. Other members of NAF's original board included Ernest Boyer, president of the Carnegie Foundation for the Advancement of Teaching; David Kearns, former chief executive officer of Xerox who later became under secretary of education; Ann McLaughlin, also a former secretary of labor; Albert Shanker, president of the American Federation of Teachers; and several top executives at American Express and other financial corporations. Phyllis Frankfort assumed the post of executive director, headquartered in New York City.

NAF's mission is to maintain the quality of programs in its network, foster expansion where there is interest on the part of industry and education, develop new academy themes, and encourage corporations generally to support development of a competitive workforce. As of 1991 NAF had state representatives in Florida, Illinois, California, New York, Maryland, Utah, Washington, and Oregon. Three schools were developing all-NAF curricula. Academies not originally sponsored by NAF may become NAF affiliates if they meet certain standards.

NAF's central office produces curriculum with input from teachers, industry, and subject matter experts. It sponsors an annual summer institute for academy teachers, meetings for academy directors, and teacher training. It raises money to provide scholarships and awards for students and teachers. It also provides administrative support and quality management.

NAF Academies have begun in two new fields: public service and manufacturing sciences. The first academies of public service opened in 1990 in Washington, D.C., and New York City. These offer two-year comprehensive programs on a model similar to the academy of finance. The Ford Academy of Manufacturing Sciences, initiated in three sites as of 1991, supplements students' regular high school program with four courses and a related internship experience. The four courses are The World of Manufacturing, Total Quality Control and Statistical Process Control (TQC and SPC), Bits and Bytes, and Manufacturing Mysteries.

Academy programs affiliated with NAF were planned or operating in twenty states plus the District of Columbia as of 1991. An NAF Academy also was operating in Mexico City. Hawaii has a statewide NAF initiative, and two other states are following suit. Enrollments in 1991 had grown to 2,980 in academy of finance programs, 904 in travel and tourism, 188 in public service, and 74 in manufacturing sciences. Enrolled students were 63 percent female, 37 percent African American, 18 percent Hispanic, and 12 percent Asian. In 1991 a total of 721 students graduated from NAF Academies; 93 percent went on to college. The large percentage going to college is seen as an unintended benefit of a program whose theme is career preparation and many of whose students are not college-bound when they enroll.

According to executive director Phyllis Frankfort, all NAF Academies share certain features:

- The curriculum focuses on one of the NAF career themes and includes NAF courses, which are revised every three years.
- Two to four teachers from different disciplines run the program as a team. They adapt the NAF curriculum to local circumstances. In some programs they have a common planning period.
- An advisory board oversees the program. It represents local businesses and school administration.
- A full-time district academy director supports the teaching teams and acts as a broker between the school and the local business community. The director reports to the advisory board, teachers, school principal, and district superintendent. If there are more than four academies in a single district, an academy coordinator at each school site may be released from teaching for one period a day.
- Teachers attend the annual NAF summer institute.
- Students are block-scheduled for at least two classes at any given time during the academy sequence.
- Business is involved locally. The advisory board for each NAF Academy must include at least five local business

members. Some programs involve local employer representatives as mentors for students. Teachers receive industry training and summer internships.

- Students obtain paid internships during the summer after their junior year. Some programs also provide after-school jobs during the senior year, as well as "shadowing" experiences.
- High expectations for students are maintained by assigning homework every day and requiring students to read a newspaper at least three times a week.
- At least one local college or university is included as a partner. Students must take at least one course for college credit during their senior year. Some begin doing so during their junior year. Some academies have formal 2+2 or 2+2+2 options linking high school with postsecondary education.
- Students represent a broad cross section of the student body, college-bound or not, who share an interest in exploring a career field. NAF requires sex equity, and also racial integration in schools with racially diverse populations, in academy enrollment. Entering students must have at least a 2.0 grade point average in English and math (or in English and social studies for the travel and tourism and public service academies).
- Half of the extra costs of the academy—for expenses such as a district coordinator, teacher training, travel by academy directors to national meetings, and field trips and other activities for students—are paid by contributions from local businesses, and half by the school system.

NAF is currently the largest network of academies. In addition to the National Diffusion Network, it has been recognized by President Bush's Education 2000 initiative, the SCANS commission (U.S. Department of Labor, 1991), and Hamilton (1990), among others. NAF academies have received awards in Maryland and in Dade County, Florida. The network has grown rapidly in recent years, and NAF intends for the growth to continue.

Washington, D.C.: A Replicated Network

Influenced in part by Philadelphia, in part by the National Academy Foundation, and in part by the success of earlier similar programs in some of its own high schools, the District of Columbia School District has adopted the academy model around which to structure programs in all of its high schools. It is doing this as part of its "Schools of Distinction" program, designed to establish at each high school in the city a special emphasis that will attract students from throughout the district (Stone, 1990).

The District of Columbia is using a two-pronged strategy: upgrading existing programs and beginning new academies where there are no existing programs on which to build. Existing programs that focus on career themes exist in six district high schools already, in the following fields: business and finance, communications, international studies, engineering, travel and tourism, and health. While these are not full-fledged academies, they provide important foundations on which to build. By adding ties to business, colleges, and government agencies, they may evolve into academies.

At the same time, plans are in place to begin academies in five high schools that lack existing career theme programs. One of the five that is already underway is the NAF public service academy, begun in the fall of 1990 at Anacostia High School. In addition to NAF sponsorship, the public service academy is also supported by the U.S. Office of Personnel Management, the National Capital Area Chapter of the American Society of Public Administration (ASPA), George Washington University, and the University of the District of Columbia. Other new academies will be started in transportation technology, leadership, environmental sciences (Earth-Tech), economics, and science.

Forty-three sophomores participated in the public service academy during the 1990–91 school year. They used a computer-based employability skills program that also taught computer and functional life skills, and they went on monthly "shadowing" field trips to various public agencies. Attendance the first year was 98 percent, compared with a school average of 60 percent, and thirteen of the eighteen students in the high school who made the honor roll were academy participants (Sinclair, 1991). NAF is helping to replicate the public service academy in other locations including New York City, Boston, San Jose, Jacksonville, and the states of New Jersey and Maine (National Academy Foundation, 1991b).

The District of Columbia Academies will be structured much like the Partnership Academies, with four core teachers (English, math, science, and social studies) and a career theme. They are designed to attract "an academically diverse student body, reflecting a wide range of ability levels [and] social and economic backgrounds" (District of Columbia Public Schools, n.d.). Their goals include stimulating students to stay in school and graduate; focusing on basic skills, problem solving, critical thinking, self-expression, and an appreciation of others; and exposing students to a wide range of positive role models. The academies' programs will include mentorships and ties to appropriate businesses and colleges. They are intended to be motivational and in some ways experimental, providing "opportunities to try new approaches for dealing with the needs of their students."

Three academies were planned for start-up in the fall of 1991:

- A health and human services academy at Eastern High School, to be associated with the Department of Health and Human Services. This is based on an existing health careers program already in place here. Louis Sullivan, secretary of the U.S. Department of Health and Human Services, has signed a Memorandum of Understanding with the district to support this Academy.
- A trans tech academy at Cardozo High School, associated with the Department of Transportation. This will involve Amtrak, Metro (the Washington, D.C., subway system), Northwest Airlines, the American Public Transit and American Trucking Associations, the Teamsters and

Transportation and Communications Unions, the Washington Regional Airports Authority, and the University of Maryland.
- A leadership academy at Spingarn High School, associated with the Departments of Defense, Treasury, and Justice; Howard University; and the American Society for Industrial Security.

All the other academies are planned to start in September 1992. All will be associated with departments of the federal government. Their focus and the departments with which they will be associated are

- Communications and technology—Department of Commerce
- Travel and tourism—Department of Commerce
- International—State Department
- Business and finance—Federal Reserve and Treasury Department
- EarthTech (environmental sciences)—Department of Energy and Environmental Protection Agency
- Economics and Science—Departments of Agriculture and the Interior

A Unified Network?

Like other movements for educational change, academies have developed networks. These play a vital role in disseminating ideas to new locations and helping people there create programs that are true to the original model. Replication also provides psychological validation for participants in existing sites, who can defend their own programs locally on the grounds that other places are copying the idea—just as new sites can defend their initiatives locally on the grounds that the idea has been successfully put into practice somewhere else. There is strength in numbers.

PHSA has raised money, provided technical assistance, and cultivated community support within the Philadelphia school district. As other cities like Washington, D.C., develop multiple academies, they may find it useful to create a local organization. In California financial support has come directly from state government, and the informal technical assistance group has supplemented the state Department of Education staff in helping new programs avoid unnecessary reinvention of wheels. On a national scale, NAF has provided psychological, technical, and material support for its member academies.

Up to now these networks have had little contact with one another. NAF Academies in California, for instance, have not been active in meetings of California Partnership Academies. Given the similarity among career academy programs, it would be logical for these networks to combine forces. However, their differences in sponsorship, history, and scale of operation may keep them separate.

FOUR

⊰ ○ ⊱

Evaluating the Academies

This chapter reviews results from evaluations of career academy programs in Philadelphia, California, and New York City. Three outcomes for students are considered: graduation from high school, subsequent employment, and participation in postsecondary education.

Evaluations to date have been seriously limited. There has not yet been any evaluation using a true experimental procedure of assigning students randomly to the academy "treatment." Such an evaluation would require encouraging enough extra students to apply to an academy so that some of them could be selected at random and the rest turned away. On the one hand, this procedure raises ethical issues. It also raises questions about how to interpret the results: if the students who are turned away perform more poorly as a result of their disappointment, the experiment will be biased toward finding positive results of the program. On the other hand, evaluations that do not use random assignment are subject to unknown biases due to possible systematic selection of students. We simply do not know the extent to which differences in outcomes between academy students and comparison groups is caused by the academy program rather than by pre-existing, unmeasured advantages of academy students.

Another limitation of existing studies is that they have not been designed to assess the relative importance of different

56

features of the academy model. The model is complex. Although some evaluations have found that academy students perform better than students in comparison groups, we have no way of knowing how much of the difference can be attributed to individual elements of the program such as the school-within-a-school structure, the integrated curriculum, the career focus, related employment, or mentors.

Description of Evaluations

Despite their limitations, existing evaluations have produced some pertinent information. In 1986–87 a study of the Philadelphia Academies was conducted by Public/Private Ventures (P/PV) (Snyder and McMullan, 1987a). This evaluation was limited to three business academies at South Philadelphia, University City, and William Penn high schools. Two kinds of information were collected. First, school records for all students who entered tenth grade in 1981 in these three programs were traced to determine whether they eventually graduated or not. Second, all 1985 graduates of the three programs were surveyed between November 1986 and March 1987. The survey collected information on demographic characteristics, employment and further education after high school, and job search activities. In addition to the business academy graduates, the survey also included two comparison groups: all graduates from the same high schools who took the non-academy business education curriculum, and a random sample of all other graduates from the three high schools.

In California the original two Peninsula Academies were evaluated from 1981 through 1986 by the American Institutes for Research (Reller, 1984, 1985, 1987). Incoming academy students at each site were matched with students from a comparison group who were similar in ethnic composition, gender, and achievement test scores. The evaluation also produced information about graduates of the program and comparison students fifteen and twenty-seven months after they graduated from high school.

Policy Analysis for California Education (PACE) evaluated the first ten California academy replications from 1985 through 1990 (Dayton, Weisberg, Stern, and Evans, 1987; Dayton, Weisberg, and Stern, 1989; Dayton and Stern, 1990, 1991; Stern and others, 1988; Stern, Dayton, Paik, and Weisberg, 1989). As in the original two Peninsula Academies, students in all but two of the replication programs were selected during the second semester of their ninth-grade year. In the two exceptional sites the Peninsula Academy model was altered to begin in ninth grade instead of tenth; accordingly, the academy students were chosen during their eighth-grade year. The selection process varied slightly from site to site but usually began by distributing information about the program to students and staff. The pool of potential enrollees was formed of students who expressed interest or who were nominated by teachers or counselors. Students were chosen from this pool if they had a record of low achievement—poor attendance, low grades, insufficient course credits—but were not more than two grade levels behind in standardized test scores. The purpose was to select students who were at high risk of not graduating on time but who appeared able to do high school work.

For the purpose of evaluation, a comparison group at each California replication site was selected during the tenth-grade year (ninth-grade year in the two sites that began the academy program in ninth grade). At each site, comparison group students came from the same school and grade level as students in the academy program. The comparison groups were selected by combing the school rosters for students whose attendance, credits, grades, and standardized test scores in the previous year resembled those of academy students. The age, gender, and race or ethnicity of comparison students were also recorded.

Students who graduated in June 1988 from eight of the California Partnership Academies were surveyed by PACE during the spring of 1989. The eight academies included the two original Peninsula Academies plus six of the replications. Graduates from the comparison group at each site were also surveyed. In the spring of 1990 students who graduated in

June 1989 were surveyed and the June 1988 graduates were surveyed for a second time.

The Philadelphia and California evaluations are quasi-experiments. They are not true experiments because students were not assigned at random to the academy and comparison groups. Instead, some academy students selected themselves, and others were nominated by teachers or counselors. Therefore, it is possible that unmeasured differences exist between the academy and comparison groups. Differences resulting from nonrandom selection might make the program appear more or less effective than it really is. For instance, if students were selected for the academy because they were thought to be bright but disaffected from school, the program would seem more effective than if disaffected students of only average or lower ability were selected. Conversely, if students selected for the academy were among the most recalcitrant or intractable in the school, the program would appear less effective than if the students selected were more docile and cooperative. Unfortunately, even statistical procedures designed to correct for selection bias (see Maddala, 1983) cannot substitute for random assignment (see LaLonde, 1986; Burtless and Orr, 1986); and, in any event, these procedures could not be applied here due to the absence of data that could be used to predict membership in the academy or the comparison group. Thus the evaluation results may to some extent reflect the consequences of selection rather than the effects of the academy program.

Recently the U.S. Department of Education sponsored a set of programs to test the effectiveness of vocational education for high school dropout prevention. Two of the programs were career academies in California. The evaluation used random assignment at several sites, but at the California sites it used nonrandom, matched comparison groups. The two California sites had the best evaluation results in the first year of the program, producing significant gains in students' academic performance and attitudes toward school (Hayward, Tallmadge, and Leu, 1991). However, possible selection bias precludes definitive causal inferences.

Finally, a follow-up survey of graduates from the academy of finance program in New York City was conducted by the Academy for Educational Development (AED) in 1990. Graduates from the program in seven high schools were interviewed. Of the 196 former students interviewed, 11 were from the program's first graduating class in 1984, and between 30 and 47 were from each of the classes that graduated in 1985 through 1989. This follow-up study did not include a comparison group.

Graduation from High School

In Philadelphia, the graduation rate among business academy students who enrolled in tenth grade in 1981 was 76.6 percent (Snyder and McMullan, 1987a, p. D-37). Unfortunately, the only figure available for comparison was a citywide graduation rate of approximately 67 percent, estimated for all students starting in grade 9. Because the two numbers were computed differently, this is only fuzzy evidence that academy students are more likely to graduate.

Stronger evidence comes from California. In the two original Peninsula Academies, Reller (1984, p. 76) reports one-year dropout rates of 2 percent in 1982–83 and 4 percent in 1983–84, compared with 10 percent and 11 percent among the comparison group students in those two years. Among seniors in 1985, Reller (1985, p. 31) reports that 94 percent graduated from the two Peninsula Academies, while only 79 percent graduated from the comparison groups. Although these are only one-year rates, this is clear evidence of higher persistence and graduation rates among academy students than among matched comparison groups.

Cumulative, multiyear dropout rates were computed for students in the California academy replications (Dayton, Weisberg, and Stern, 1989). Among students who entered as sophomores in the fall of 1985, the three-year dropout rate was 7.3 percent in the academies and 14.6 percent in the comparison groups. For the cohort entering in the fall of 1986, the two-year dropout rate was 6.6 percent in the academies and 14.3 percent in the comparison groups. Among students who enrolled as sophomores in the fall of 1987, the dropout rate that year was 2.8 percent in the academies and 2.2 percent in the comparison groups. Except in this last cohort, which was observed for only one year, the academy dropout rates are substantially lower.

Lower dropout rates among academy students in the California replication sites followed several years of improved performance in school (Stern and others, 1988; Stern, Dayton, Paik, and Weisberg, 1989). While enrolled in the academies, students recorded better attendance, failed fewer courses, earned more credits, and obtained better grades than did the students in comparison groups. Higher graduation rates therefore occurred as a culmination of these cumulative results.

A benefit-cost analysis was done for students who entered the California replication academies as sophomores in the fall of 1985 (Stern, Dayton, Paik, and Weisberg, 1989). This was the only cohort the evaluation followed from grades 10 through 12. Program benefits were the additional expected lifetime earnings obtained by academy students as a result of the fact that their high school graduation rate was higher than the comparison group's. These amounted to approximately $2.5 million (discounted) for this cohort of 327 students. Program costs were the additional teachers' time, corporate volunteers' time, and other real resources used by the academies. The total cost to society as a whole for academy students in this cohort was approximately $1.2 million (including the time of corporate volunteers); the cost to taxpayers was about $0.75 million (excluding corporate volunteers' time). The estimated net benefit from dropout prevention was therefore $1.3 million for society as a whole, or $1.75 million for taxpayers.

Employment After Graduation from High School

As described above, the P/PV evaluation in Philadelphia surveyed business academy graduates from three high schools, along with graduates of the regular business education curriculum and a random sample of all other graduates from the same three schools. Both the academy and other business education groups contained significantly larger proportions of females—83 and 80 percent, respectively—than the random sample from the high schools at large, which was 53 percent female. The proportion of black students in the academy, 91 percent, was also significantly larger than among the other business graduates and the random sample of all graduates, which were 79 percent and 75 percent black, respectively (Snyder and McMullan, 1987a, p. D-42).

Both the business academy and other business program graduates were significantly more likely to be employed at the time of the survey, and on average they had been employed a larger fraction of the time since graduation, compared to the sample of all graduates (Snyder and McMullan, 1987a, p. D-45). Among employed students, both groups of business graduates were employed significantly more often in clerical occupations, but the three samples did not differ significantly in hourly pay or average hours worked per week. A significantly larger fraction of business academy graduates worked for companies that were official business academy sponsors (Snyder and McMullan, 1987a, pp. D-49, 50). According to Snyder and McMullan, "Since these companies represent many of the 'blue chip' employers in the city, this advantage is substantial" (p. D-51).

Graduates from the original two California Peninsula Academies in 1984, and from matched comparison groups in the same two high schools, were followed for twenty-seven months after graduation (Reller, 1987). No significant differences between Academy and comparison students were found in employment status, wages, or hours worked.

Labor market outcomes from the Spring 1989 survey of June 1988 graduates from the original two Peninsula Academies and six replication sites are shown in Table 4.1. Labor market outcomes from the Spring 1990 survey of June 1988 and June 1989 graduates are also shown. The two surveys cover slightly different populations of former students because two of the 1989 survey sites were replaced in 1990 by two other sites.

**Table 4.1. Main Current Activity, and Job Characteristics,
of California Partnership Academy and Comparison Graduates.**

1989 Survey (1988 Graduates)	Academy (n=142) Percentage of participation	Comparison (n=91)
Main activity		
Going to school	64	64
Working, not in military	63	71
In the military	8	4
Neither school nor work	6	9
How employment was obtained (working students only)		
School	17	11
Public or private agency	4	3
Employer directly	38	38
Relative or friend	41	48
Mean hours worked per week (working students only)	31.2	27.9
Mean current hourly wage (working students only)	$5.66	$5.56

Source: Adapted from Dayton and Stern, 1990, pp. 7, 12, 13.

1990 Survey (1988 and 1989 Graduates)	Academy (n=205) Percentage of participation	Comparison (n=215)
Main activity		
Going to school	61	66
Working, not in military	69	66
In the military	6	4
Neither school nor work	4	4
How employment was obtained (working students only)		
School	18	7
Public or private agency	9	4
Employer directly	38	40
Relative or friend	34	48
Mean hours worked per week (working students only)	31.5	27.9
Mean current hourly wage (working students only)	$6.57	$6.75

Source: Adapted from Dayton and Stern, 1991, pp. 10, 11, 17, 18.

Table 4.1 shows similar patterns of activity for the academy and comparison groups. In both years, approximately two-thirds of the students were employed in civilian jobs at the time of the survey. The proportion who were neither working nor in school was less than 10 percent in the first year, and less than 5 percent in the second year. Differences between the academy and comparison groups are not statistically significant.

Some statistically significant differences do appear in the job characteristics shown in Table 4.1 for students who were employed at the time of the survey. More academy graduates reported finding their jobs through school rather than through relatives or friends. This difference is statistically significant in the 1990 survey. It indicates that academies provided extra help in finding jobs for graduates.

Table 4.1 also shows that academy graduates work significantly more hours per week than the comparison group. For both years the difference, on average, is about three hours; this is statistically significant. This same average three-hour difference exists whether the graduates are attending postsecondary school or not.

The pattern of differences in hourly wages is more complicated. In the 1989 survey, there was a significant advantage in both starting and current wages for academy graduates who were currently enrolled in postsecondary school, relative to comparison group students who were also enrolled in school (Dayton and Stern, 1990). However, among those who were not in school, academy graduates were currently earning significantly less than the comparison group. In the 1990 survey, academy and comparison graduates who were still in school earned about the same current wage, but among those who were out of school the comparison students earned more (Dayton and Stern, 1991). Apparently, being an academy graduate and being enrolled in postsecondary school interact positively in determining current wages. However, combining in-school and out-of-school graduates, Table 4.1 shows no significant difference in wages between academy and comparison graduates in California.

The wage differences in Table 4.1 can be adjusted for the fact that the follow-up surveys included only graduates, not dropouts. As Reller (1987) points out, since the high school graduation rate was higher in the academy than in the comparison group, and since dropouts on average fare worse in the labor market, excluding dropouts biases the follow-up evaluation against the academies. Unlike the bias due to initial selection of academy students, which could lead to either over- or underestimation of academy effects on school performance, the bias Reller notes in the follow-up studies will most likely lead to underestimation of benefits produced by academies.

We can adjust the observed wage differences by using other data to estimate dropouts' average wages. The best source for this data is the National Longitudinal Survey of Youth (NLSY). As of 1980–82 the average difference in wages between recent high school graduates and dropouts was $0.73 per hour (Stern, Paik, Catterall, and Nakata, 1989). Updating this for inflation would make this $1.08 per hour in 1989 dollars. Subtracting $1.08 from the average wages of academy and comparison graduates would give estimates of $4.58 and $4.48 for average wages of dropouts from the two groups, respectively, in the 1989 survey. Then, using the fact that the academy and comparison group dropout rates were 7 and 14 percent in this cohort, we can compute an estimated average wage for dropouts and graduates combined. The estimated combined average wage is found to be $5.58 for academy students and $5.41 for the comparison group. This is a difference of $0.17, compared to the observed difference of $0.10 between academy and comparison group graduates only. As expected, correcting for the bias increases the difference between the academy and comparison group, although not much.

The 1990 California survey asked students whether their current jobs were "related to any specialized courses you took in high school." Among the 1989 graduates, 55 percent of the academy students answered this question affirmatively, as opposed to 28 percent of the comparison group. This difference is statistically significant. It indicates that academy students are following a more coherent career path as they make the transition from school to work.

In New York City, a follow-up of 196 graduates from the academy of finance program in seven high schools discovered that 68 percent were working at the time of the survey, 21 percent were looking for a job, and 10 percent were not working or seeking work (Academy for Educational Development, 1990). Since many of these respondents were still in college (see the following section), these figures do not reflect the employment they will probably attain in a few more years. Of those who had jobs, 20 percent reported working in financial services, and an additional 28 percent were working in a related field such as accounting, business, or economics. Most of the employed graduates were working more than thirty hours a week. Seventy-seven percent were earning $7.00 or more per hour, and 39 percent were making at least $10.00 per hour. Not surprisingly, full-time work and high wages were more common among graduates who had been out longer. There was no comparison group in this evaluation, so it is not possible to estimate how well these individuals would have done in the absence of the academy program.

Participation in Postsecondary Schooling

One purpose of career academies is to preserve the possibility that students can continue on to college. Some academies emphasize this more than others.

In the follow-up study of graduates from the Philadelphia business academy, 64 percent of the academy graduates said their main activity was working, and 18 percent indicated school was their main activity. These proportions are significantly different from the sample of all graduates, of whom 42 percent said they were principally engaged in work and 35 percent said school (Snyder and McMullan, 1987a, p. D-45). Similarly, among those who had ever enrolled in postsecondary education, 54 percent of the academy graduates said their degree objective was a vocational certificate and 14 percent said a bachelor's degree. These proportions are significantly different from the 36 percent who intended to get certificates and the 43 percent who intended to get bachelor's degrees among the sample of all graduates (Snyder and McMullan, 1987a, p. D-47). Graduates from non-academy business programs were more similar to academy graduates than to the sample of all graduates in their answers to these questions. These results are consistent with the primary goals of the business academy in Philadelphia—namely, keeping students in high school and preparing them for employment after graduation. Although academic and vocational courses are to some extent coordinated in the business academy, preparation for college is not a major goal.

In the follow-up of graduates from the original two California Peninsula Academies fifteen months after graduation, Reller (1987, p. 25) found that the rate of enrollment in postsecondary schooling among academy graduates, 62 percent, was higher than the 47 percent among the comparison group. The proportion both in school and working was 51 percent among the academy graduates and 34 percent among the comparison group. At the twenty-seven-month follow-up, the educational objectives of academy graduates were significantly higher than those of the comparison group, with 55 percent expecting to complete a four-year degree or more, versus 22 percent in the comparison group (Reller, 1987, p. 41).

Results on postsecondary schooling from the 1989 and 1990 surveys of California career academy graduates are shown in Table 4.2. There are no consistent differences between academy and comparison graduates. Roughly 70 to 80 percent of those who are enrolled in school attend two-year colleges. Between 70 and 80 percent also say they intend to get a four-year or graduate degree. The percentage who expect to acquire a master's or doctoral degree is significantly larger (33 percent) among the comparison group than among academy graduates (16 percent) in the 1990 survey, but the 1989 survey found a slight difference in the opposite direction.

Table 4.2. Postsecondary Schooling of California Partnership Academy and Comparison Graduates Attending School at Time of Survey.

1989 Survey (1988 Graduates)	Academy (n=89) Percentage of participation	Comparison (n=56)
Type of school attended		
Adult night school	1	2
Vocational or business school	8	0
Community college	68	81
Four-year college	24	14
Highest level of education expected		
Vocational certificate	4	7
Two-year degree	18	19
Four-year degree	60	59
Postbaccalaureate degree	19	15
Enrolled full time	77	74
Receiving financial aid	27	9

Source: Adapted from Dayton and Stern, 1990, pp. 9–11.

1990 Survey (1988 and 1989 Graduates)	Academy (n=124) Percentage of participation	Comparison (n=138)
Type of school attended		
Adult night school	1	1
Vocational or business school	11	8
Community college	73	76
Four-year college	15	15
Highest level of education expected		
Vocational certificate	7	4
Two-year degree	15	12
Four-year degree	61	52
Postbaccalaureate degree	16	33
Enrolled full-time	72	80
Receiving financial aid	16	17

Source: Adapted from Dayton and Stern, 1991, pp. 13, 14, 16.

Again we can adjust for the fact that dropouts were excluded from the follow-up survey. Table 4.1 showed that 64 percent of both academy and comparison graduates from 1988 were attending school. We know that in this cohort the dropout rate was 7 percent from the academies and 14 percent from the comparison groups. If we assume that no dropouts were attending postsecondary school in 1989, then the percentage of all academy students (graduates and dropouts combined) attending school in 1989 would be 60 percent. Among all comparison group students it would be 55 percent. Again this increases the difference between academy and comparison students, but not much.

Evaluation of the academy of finance in New York City found very high rates of college attendance (Academy for Educational Development, 1990). Eighty-nine percent of graduates in the follow-up survey said they had attended a four-year college or university, and another 3 percent had attended a two-year college. One-third had completed their degrees. Finance or business was the major field of study for 58 percent of those who attended college, and 67 percent planned to pursue a master's degree or doctorate. Evidently the academy of finance has been successful in supporting students' desire for further education, though the same students might have gone on to college even without the academy program.

Summary of Evaluation Results

High school career academies have various goals. In the Philadelphia and California academies, dropout prevention has been a primary goal, and there is evidence that this purpose has been achieved. Evaluations in California found academy students performed better in school than comparison groups from the same high schools and a larger proportion of academy students received their high school diplomas. A benefit-cost analysis of some of the California academies indicates that the additional expected lifetime income of academy graduates who would otherwise have dropped out is more than sufficient by itself to justify the additional cost of the program.

The California evidence indicates that some additional benefits are derived in the form of additional hours worked by academy graduates relative to comparison groups. Graduates from the California academies also are just as likely to attend postsecondary schooling as graduates in their comparison groups. These findings imply that dropout prevention was not obtained by delivering a watered-down high school curriculum. While inducing some would-be dropouts to finish high school, academies have provided no worse preparation for employment and continued schooling after high school. Similarly, in Philadelphia, a survey of academy graduates six months after their June 1990 graduation found 89 percent were either employed, serving in the military, or continuing their education; and an eighteen-month follow-up of academy graduates from the class of 1989 found 88 percent in at least one of these categories (Philadelphia High School Academies, 1991).

The academy model is evolving. Newer academies, such as the health academies in Philadelphia and in Oakland, California, as well as the academy of finance, have put more emphasis on maintaining students' option to attend college. Their focal themes orient students toward occupational sectors in which there is much room for upward mobility through further education (for example, in health or financial services) in contrast to occupations achievable through traditional vocational education (such as secretarial work and electrical trades), where opportunities for advancement are more limited. These newer programs have demonstrated that the academy model can be effective in preparing students for four-year colleges.

The evaluations also suggest that it is possible to achieve the goals of dropout prevention and college preparation at the same time, in the same program. Some of the California academies, whose students were selected in ninth grade because they showed early warning signs of dropping out, have been able not only to retain those students through high school but also to equip them to attend four-year colleges. It is not realistic to expect all students to go to college, but it is important that academies keep that option open, so that they will not be stigmatized as second-rate programs for the "non–college-bound."

While existing evaluating results are suggestive and promising, we must repeat their limitations. No career academy has yet been evaluated by a true experimental, random-assignment procedure. Although the California evaluations used a relatively rigorous, quasi-experimental design, it is still possible that unknown selection effects account for some or all of the findings. Moreover, existing evaluations have not tried to test which of the academies' various features make the most difference. When we offer advice in the following chapters about how to run an academy, our judgments therefore must rely on our interpretation of experience in the programs we have operated, visited, or heard about.

Part Two:

Creating
a
Career Academy

⊷ ○ ⊶

FIVE

Procedures, Problems, and Principles

This chapter offers guidance on how to establish a career academy based on the California Partnership Academy model. First we describe a set of tasks that must be accomplished to get the program going. Next we discuss possible problems that should be anticipated. In the last section we articulate some guiding principles to preserve the integrity of the program and the commitment of its participants.

Starting an Academy

A district interested in starting a partnership academy should begin by performing a feasibility study to determine how many students need the program and whether local businesses will provide enough jobs, mentors, and other necessary resources. The district superintendent should be directly associated with the efforts to initiate the program in order to gain the required support in the schools and at the upper levels of the business community. The feasibility study provides information for choosing the academy's career focus. There are two major issues here. The first is whether businesses will offer entry-level jobs that provide for a career path with upward mobility. Unskilled work does not provide the motivation for students to become proficient in their academic and vocational subjects. The second is whether the school district can develop a vocational/technical curriculum for the career area. This is dependent on the availability of the requisite teaching staff, equipment, and facilities. The initial assessment can be done by a district administrator and selected individuals representing the business partners. After these questions have been satisfactorily answered, funding for program development should be sought.

Developmental Tasks

The first and most important steps in developing an academy are to select a program director and to create the implementation plan. The director is responsible for creating the plan and guiding the efforts of the teaching staff as they attempt to make the program operational. Consequently, the director must be respected by both the district administration and the teaching staff for his or her management skills and curriculum expertise. During the first three to four years of operation, until the program is institutionalized, it is usually best if the academy director is a district administrator familiar with district policies and state education codes. This individual might be the director of vocational education, director of state and federal projects, or curriculum director. The director needs a significant amount of expertise and influence to be able to negotiate resources, teachers, facilities, and assistance from the district office and from the business community. A district administrator also will be aware of sources for operational funds, such as the Carl D. Perkins Vocational and Applied Technology Education Act (U.S. Congress, 1990), the Education Consolidation and Improvement Act (ECIA), and appropriate state and local resources. If academies are to be established at more than one school in a district, it is necessary to have a district administrator as academies director to control competition for resources and to minimize costs caused by duplication of efforts. An entrepreneurial spirit in the director is desirable.

Since academies are integral parts of a school district's secondary program, planning must be coordinated with the school's calendar. Preliminary planning should begin the year before the program accepts students. The implementation plan should specify all the activities that must be accomplished for the academy to become operational. It should at least describe the following tasks and assign responsibilities for their completion:

- Management
- Budget
- Staffing
- Student selection
- The school-within-a-school format
- Curriculum
- Counseling
- Parental involvement
- Business commitment and resources

A suggested schedule for the planning year is given in Table 5.1.

Management

The partnership must assemble a committed group of administrators, lead teachers, and business personnel to organize

Table 5.1. A Schedule for the Planning Year.

Date	Activity
September to November	Select director and conduct feasibility study
November	Submit proposal to state
February	Receive notification of award
February to March	Develop plan, identify staff, form advisory committee, and develop budget
March to April	Recruit and select students
May to August	Plan motivational activities (speakers, field trips, and awards)
June to August	Develop curriculum, secure equipment, prepare facilities

and manage the academies. Commitment is required because of the nature of the students and the array of difficult problems they will encounter. The academy director must work closely with the teachers, school site administrators, and business representatives to develop and operate the program.

Most academies have an advisory committee consisting of the academy director, the school principals, the academy department chairpersons, the work experience coordinators, and representatives from local businesses. The academy director establishes the advisory committee and creates the budget. The advisory committee reviews the plan, the proposed budget, and the progress of development. It provides a forum for communication between the members of the partnership.

The academy's director and department chairpersons do most of the day-to-day planning and management of the program. In addition, task forces may be formed to deal with short-term concerns or handle particular components such as scheduling, equipment acquisition, student recruitment and selection, curriculum development, mentors, and work experience. Task force members are usually the department chairpersons, vice principals, academy teachers, work experience coordinator, and appropriate individuals from business.

Budget

The budget must present a complete and realistic cost picture. This includes initial capital costs, planning costs, and incremental costs of the academy program over the regular academic program. Capital costs include equipment acquisition and facility modifications. The equipment costs depend primarily on the technical focus of the academy. For example, a computer academy may require a computer work station for each student, while a health academy may require extensive laboratory equipment. If major equipment purchases are made, initial capital costs may amount to $50,000 or $75,000. Most school sites need some room modifications, such as security systems to protect valuable equipment. It may be necessary to purchase work tables, build cabinets, or move walls.

California provides planning grants of $15,000 to cover the six- to eight-month planning phase of the program. These funds pay for teachers to be released from their classrooms to serve on the task forces, develop curriculum, visit established academies, and attend the annual statewide academies conference.

Ongoing incremental costs may include expenditures for an additional common preparation period for each teacher, reduction in class size, instructional aides, staff development, curriculum development, and maintenance of equipment. The amounts vary depending primarily on the salaries of the staff. They normally range from $750 to $1,000 per student per year in a fully implemented partnership academy (Stern, Dayton, Paik, and Weisberg, 1989). The total incremental costs for an academy, with two classes each of sophomores, juniors, and seniors, is roughly $100,000 to $150,000 per year. After the budget is agreed upon, the academy director must find a way to obtain the resources from district-controlled funds; from state, federal, and foundation funds; and from the business partnership.

Staffing

Among the most important factors in the success of an academy is the relationship between its teaching staff and the students, parents, and other staff members. Recruiting an academy staff must be done with care. The selection of the academy chairperson, or lead teacher, at the school site is almost as important as the selection of the district director. The site chairperson must manage day-to-day operation of the academy, negotiate with the principal over scheduling issues, and lead the implementation of the program at the school. The chairperson must be sensitive to the legitimate concerns of the school's non-academy faculty regarding resources and alert the director to problems as they arise.

Each school's principal and academy chairperson select the remainder of the teaching staff. They must choose committed and skilled teachers who are sensitive to the special needs of at-risk students and are willing to devote the extra time and energy necessary to help these students succeed. Teachers volunteer to work in the program. Their selection is based on their enthusiasm and their ability to guide and motivate at-risk students and to function as part of an interdisciplinary team. Academy teachers must be committed to using success-oriented instructional techniques, working together to develop integrated subject matter, using new technology, and working with employers. They must understand that academies have to maintain standards, and they must demand that students perform accordingly.

Core academy staff are assigned to the program on a full-time basis so that they can work with the same students for more than one year. It is best to seek a balance of male and female, young and mature teachers. Every effort should be made to recruit teachers who reflect the racial and ethnic diversity of the students and are bilingual if limited-English-proficient students are present. Desirable skills for academy teachers include

- Ability to work with others as part of a team
- Interpersonal skills in dealing with students and parents
- Interest in interdisciplinary curriculum development
- Willingness to upgrade teaching methods
- Interest in the use of technology as a teaching and learning tool
- Ability to motivate at-risk students to a high level of achievement
- Willingness to share decision making with employers

An instructional aide to function as a technical assistant in the laboratory classroom is a valuable addition to the program. Typical duties include helping teachers with classroom management and equipment, providing individualized help to students, correcting papers, entering grades, and tutoring students. Instructional aides also can inform new students about such matters as attendance requirements, academic expectations, availability of school resources, and behavior expectations. In programs in which there are significant numbers of limited-English-proficient students, this position is usually filled by an individual fluent in the dominant language.

Some academies use part of the aide's time for parent outreach. This is particularly useful when the students are limited English proficient and the aide speaks the dominant language, or when many students are concentrated in a particular neighborhood. Aides coordinate parent/teacher conferences, follow up with parents whose students are truant, and encourage parents to visit classes.

The academy work experience coordinator is the major liaison with business. The position is usually the responsibility of an academy teacher, but it may be filled by a retiree or a loaned employee paid for by business. The coordinator visits the business partners to obtain commitments for mentors, determine the number and appropriateness of jobs available, and monitor students in the workplace. Duties of the coordinator include

- Managing the mentor program
- Obtaining jobs for all eligible students
- Providing job orientation workshops for students
- Monitoring the workplace environment to check its appropriateness
- Serving as a liaison between classroom teachers and job supervisors
- Reviewing evaluations from employers on student performance
- Gathering feedback from students on their work experience

Selection of Students

Recruitment of the target population for each academy's tenth-grade class begins during the spring semester of the ninth grade. California legislation for the partnership academies defines as eligible students who have three or more of the following characteristics:

- A record of underachievement shown by grades and teacher or counselor judgment
- Irregular attendance
- A low level of interest in the regular academic program
- Economic or educational disadvantage
- Interest in the academy program, willingness to change study and attendance habits, and motivation to start on a career path.

The program was not conceived for students with serious emotional or behavioral problems. In addition, academies staffs have not had much success with students whose reading and math test scores are more than three years below grade level. Exceptions can be made and students admitted to the program if the staff decides that the test scores do not adequately reflect the student's potential.

Academy teachers actively recruit in the noncollege preparatory classes, where the target population is most likely to be found. Students and staff are informed of the recruitment process by notices in their respective bulletins. Academy staff make ten- to fifteen-minute presentations in lower- or general-track classrooms, such as general math. In these presentations, the teachers are careful to avoid stigmatizing the students or program by using such pejorative terms as *dropout* or *disadvantaged.* Instead they emphasize the positive aspects of the program. They describe the school-within-a-school format, the difference between the academy coursework and regular coursework, and the benefits of being in the academies. These benefits include jobs in good companies with good salaries, mentors, field trips, speakers, special events, smaller classes, and the esprit de corps of the students and teachers.

Teachers must be certain students fully understand the strict nature of the program: contact with the home; a demanding schedule with little room for electives; the same classmates for four periods of the day; the same teachers for two to three years; and stringent requirements for attendance, punctuality, behavior, and performance. Some academies mail monthly evaluation reports for each class to the parents. These evaluations are based on attendance, attitude, behavior, and academic performance. The reports emphasize the positive and are kept as a cumulative record. Students are made to understand that they will not be recommended for a work experience position until all their teachers agree that they have met academy standards. This is an important incentive since students enter the program with the expectation that they will have access to good entry-level jobs during their senior year.

The School-Within-a-School Format

Academies are organized as schools-within-schools. They operate as a part of comprehensive high schools but are kept small by design. The resulting family-like atmosphere and the assignment of students to the same teachers for three years allows teachers to become familiar with each student's background. This gives responsibility for each student's educational development to teachers who can relate to each as an individual.

The structure of the school-within-a-school allows the staff considerable freedom to develop the program, which leads to curriculum experimentation and program adjustment to meet student needs. Time can be used flexibly to accommodate team teaching, guest speakers, field trips, and parent conferences. Academy teachers as a group establish policies and procedures for attendance, homework, grading, and parent conferences.

Integrated Curriculum

The academy program is built on a solid academic foundation. Its success depends on a rigorous curriculum designed to support the career focus. The curriculum's major objectives are to provide

- Integrated academic and vocational/technical coursework that demonstrates the relevance of academics to the workplace

- Motivation to succeed by using success-oriented instructional strategies
- Employability skills required for job placement and career advancement
- Technical training that prepares students for jobs in industry immediately upon graduation
- Advanced technical training and preparation for college

The curriculum is integrated horizontally across the academic and vocational/technical subjects and vertically to build toward graduation, workplace readiness, and possible postsecondary education. It has strong career-planning components that provide career awareness, exploration, and guidance. Students are taught how to research a company or a college, fill out applications, and interview. They prepare résumés; interview one another; and have their interview techniques critiqued by one another, by their teachers, and sometimes by their mentors or other industry representatives. The curriculum is modified as necessary to adapt to the range of student abilities and to meet the requirements of business. Standards are maintained, and students are made to understand that these standards prepare them not only for their first jobs but for advancement in the workforce.

Counseling

In most academies teachers serve as guidance advisors. The students require constant monitoring to improve their attendance, raise their grades, and make significant progress toward meeting graduation requirements. Academy teachers try to promote students' motivation, ethical development, self-esteem, and conflict resolution and communication skills. The employability skills component of the curriculum emphasizes honesty, integrity, tolerance of differences, and fairness.

School counselors work with academy teachers to help students select their non-academy courses and to provide career and postsecondary educational guidance. Seniors who plan to continue their education are helped with college selection and recommendations. When necessary, counselors refer students to community agencies. These agencies provide professional counseling to help students cope with personal problems, such as substance abuse and dysfunctional families, that affect their attitudes toward their peers, classwork, and attendance.

Involving Parents

Academies make every effort to gain the support of students' families to reaffirm them as partners in the education process. Prospective students and their families are invited to an evening meeting with the academy staff and the director, during which the program is explained and questions are answered. Teachers speak informally about their respective courses, and the academy chairperson explains students' and parents' responsibilities. Parents are informed of the academic and behavioral requirements and made aware of the counseling and other support services available to academy students and their families. They are asked to make a commitment to provide an area for study where possible, ensure that their students do their homework on time, attend academy functions and ceremonies, and support the program. Parents may be asked to sign a contract that signifies their intent to comply with these requirements before their student is accepted into the academy. The contract lists academy goals and objectives and program expectations of students. When necessary, translators attend the meetings and the contracts are written in the dominant languages as well as English.

There is careful monitoring of and frequent reporting to parents on individual student performance and attendance. Parents are expected to participate in student conferences when problems such as truancy arise. All the student's teachers attend these meetings. Parents and students are impressed when three or four teachers take the time to show that much interest in them. Parents are informed when the problems are resolved. They are encouraged to visit classes and to participate actively in the academy's award ceremonies and other school affairs.

Business Commitment and Resources

Business has important roles in the development and operation of an academy. It provides specifications for particular skills required by the workplace, entry-level jobs, resources (funds, equipment, and mentors), and assistance with enhancement activities (speakers, award ceremonies, and facility tours).

Eleventh-grade students are matched with mentors from the business community. Training sessions for both mentors and students are invaluable before they meet. Both are encouraged to consider what they expect from the relationship and asked to set a goal for their time together. Mentoring relationships must be monitored at the school site. Teachers should watch for relationships that are not working and be ready to change mentors if necessary.

Work experience is an integral part of the curriculum. Academy students learn that academic achievement has value beyond school. Work experience demonstrates the connection of academic work to the world outside.

Enrichment activities provided by the partnership with business further reinforce the academic environment. These include mentoring, field trips, speakers from industry, and site tours of participating companies. Awards and ceremonies that highlight student achievement are frequent—for example, pizza luncheons for "Students of the Month." Parents and mentors are invited to these events. Recognition of student achievement demonstrates the positive approach used in the academies to build self-esteem in the students. Instead of penalizing them for doing something wrong, the academies take the proactive stance of rewarding students for doing something right. Usually these events represent the first positive recognition these students have received in high school. The ceremonies also emphasize the importance of parent participation and support.

Potential Problems

The partnership academy model is complex, and it differs significantly from standard procedure in most high schools.

Therefore, problems naturally arise. These tend to cluster around academy staff's relationship with other school staff, student recruitment, integrating the academic and vocational curricula, maintaining the business partnership, and funding. Here we discuss these problems and suggest possible solutions or options derived from the experiences of various academies.

Staff Interaction

California Partnership Academies have been designed primarily to serve students who appear at risk of not finishing high school. The ever-increasing numbers of at-risk youth have prompted educators to ask, and rightly so, why the academy program cannot be expanded to serve more students. Why should only academies be kept small and given the resources to reduce class size and (often) add an extra preparation period for its teachers when other teachers are also serving educationally disadvantaged students? Many students who are performing well in high school could also benefit from a career academy program. The situation is especially bad in California, where the pupil-to-teacher ratio is very high. As a result, the attitude of non-academy faculty can range from neutral to antagonistic. Some staff become vocal fault finders. This problem can pose a real threat to academies.

Negative feelings are exacerbated if an academy does not select enough disadvantaged and difficult-to-educate students, leaving them to be taught in the regular high school. One academy teacher keeps her roll book handy to show complaining colleagues just who her students are and then asks if they would like them back. This ends the discussion with those who know the students and the problems they have caused in the past.

Academies have taken various approaches to maintaining good relations with their non-academy colleagues. At the autumn pre-school faculty meetings some academies ask for the cooperation and support of the non-academy school personnel. The academy chairperson reviews the program's goals, administrative structure, and funding sources to encourage the staff to see the program as a contribution to their school's offerings, not as competition for scarce resources. Some academies invite the rest of the faculty to a breakfast or informal luncheon once a year. Still others invite the school's staff to attend when the students report on their summer work experiences. Seeing the students' pride in their accomplishments is frequently a moving experience that helps the non-academy staff realize the benefits of the program for these at-risk students.

Even after the funding sources for the program are explained, many teachers find it difficult to believe that the cost of academies does not detract from the district's regular programs. Teacher union representatives must be made to understand the extra responsibilities that each academy teacher carries, so that they do not feel the academy staff are receiving special treatment. It is important to explain that their responsibilities go well beyond the normal duties of a teacher. Unless academy teachers are given sufficient time to handle the extra work of establishing the school-within-a-school structure and coordinating the involvement with business, they become overwhelmed and frustrated. The common extra preparation period is particularly important during the first three years while teachers are developing the initial version of the curriculum. Even with the extra time a few academy teachers leave the program because of the strain of additional work. Some teachers also find it stressful to be emotionally involved with the same at-risk teenagers for three years. As one observed, "When you have students for one year they are on your mind. If you keep them for three years, they are on your conscience."

Academy staffs have on occasion developed an uncooperative spirit toward the administration and other faculty. The academy director must check for signs of abuse of privilege or an inappropriate sense of power. Any temptation by an academy staff to think it is empowered to ignore the legitimate needs and wishes of the site administration must be avoided. The staff of one academy thought that because of their school-within-a-school status they did not have to follow the direction of a new principal. Their attitude resulted in a dismantled team and an academy in disarray.

Student Selection

When the entire recruitment process is faithfully followed, students seldom leave the program, either voluntarily or involuntarily. The recruitment process ensures that students and parents understand the academic and behavioral demands the program places on students. As an example, one program was not funded until midsummer, so the regular recruitment process could not be followed the first year. Students were chosen on the basis of poor grades, absenteeism, and lack of credits, but they were not required to make a commitment to the program. As a result, teachers found it very difficult to attain satisfactory results with these students. More students than usual left voluntarily, and others were dropped from the program. It was also difficult to recruit the second year, since the program was stigmatized as being exclusively for students who were difficult to teach. The academy staff worked on emphasizing positive aspects of the program, and in the third year it succeeded in recruiting students who understood the commitment they were expected to make. Since then the recruitment problem has disappeared, and there is now a waiting list of students wanting to enter the program.

One strength of the academy is that it is voluntary. If a student decides to leave, he or she can return to the regular school. Students who are disruptive, or who refuse to study or come to class regularly, are counseled and then put on contract. If the inappropriate behavior does not stop, they are dropped from the program. Dropping students who refuse to measure up to academy standards sends the message to the entire class that inappropriate behavior will not be tolerated. Academies are forced to take this tough stance. The program cannot survive with the business community if ill-behaved students are sent to fill the job slots. Business cannot afford workers with poor performance and attendance records. Academy students are told, "If you like the job you have, thank a graduate: his or her success in the workplace gave the program a good name and paved the way for you."

Curriculum

The academy curriculum must be kept rigorous. Sometimes teachers with the empathy needed to work with at-risk students make the mistake of lowering their performance expectations. They are so anxious to make the students feel successful that they demand too little. While students may respond positively at first, they soon may start to take advantage of the situation. Standards must be maintained and high achievement demanded from the moment the students enter the program.

Developing an integrated curriculum is not an easy or a straightforward task. There is no standard procedure. Teachers attempting to develop an integrated curriculum ask many questions. How does the technical course relate to English? How do you handle the broad range of student abilities, particularly when so many are behind in their coursework? How do you align the curriculum with employers' demands?

The knowledge base for developing an integrated academy curriculum grows every year, but it is an iterative process that requires many alterations and revisions and technical input from the business advisory committees. The annual statewide academies conference in California helps by providing a forum in which teachers from the different sites can share lessons and instructional methods. The academies technical assistance committee is working to enable teachers to share lessons via electronic mail on existing networks.

Another question asked by students, parents, and teachers is whether the curriculum satisfies college requirements. The emphasis on academics in the academy curriculum undoubtedly gives the students a stronger background than they would have had otherwise. However, if students wish to take such pre-college requirements as foreign language, they must do so outside the program. Although it is theoretically possible, students usually cannot be expected to complete entrance requirements for four-year colleges if they enter the academy program far behind in course credits. Such students ordinarily attend community college first.

Block-scheduling of students to fit the school-within-a-school structure and to give academy teachers a common preparation period can cause scheduling problems. It is important for the student recruitment effort to be completed early in the year, so that academy students can be entered into the master schedule before the rest of the students. One of the two peninsula academies almost did not begin on time because the instructional vice principal was unable to figure out how to fit the academy program into her carefully crafted master schedule. Plans for the program came to a standstill until an enterprising teacher in the program offered to enter the students into the computer himself. He showed her how it could be done without destroying her schedule. Adding the special academy features to the existing conflicting requirements of a high school master schedule can be daunting. It requires supportive administrative and counseling staffs who are willing to negotiate solutions.

The Business Partnership

Developing and maintaining the school-business partnership present several major problems for which it is difficult to discover general solutions. While academies can begin the first year without substantial business support, serious problems develop in the second and third years when the mentors and work experience are required. If students have been promised mentors and jobs and do not receive them, they will quickly become disillusioned.

The business liaison role is crucial to the solution of any of these problems. The important first question is who will be the business liaison. When the Peninsula Academies began, the Mid-Peninsula Urban Coalition took on this role. After the coalition phased out of the program, maintaining the relationship with business presented a problem. Teachers in the Peninsula Academies assumed the responsibility, but they had the advantage of using contacts developed by the coalition. Their willingness to perform the liaison function may have been partly due to the glamour of working with the high-tech Silicon Valley companies that supported the program. Developing this relationship can be much more difficult in areas that do not have large, well-established sponsorship.

Most teachers do not want to be burdened with the responsibilities of the business liaison. Their profession is teaching, and good teaching plus developing the integrated curriculum, counseling students, and meeting with parents takes all their time and energy. One promising practice is to involve the school's work experience coordinator in the academies. Work experience coordinators are knowledgeable about jobs in the local area. One program employs a retired school administrator to handle some of the jobs coordination and mentor responsibilities and relies on the work experience coordinator at the school to handle the rest. In another program, the participating businesses contribute to a fund that provides an individual from the business sector to act as liaison. Use of business retirees is another promising practice. There are a growing number of energetic retirees who might welcome the opportunity to help high school students. In addition, business retirees are knowledgeable about how to approach their former colleagues and gain commitment to the program.

A major task for the business liaison individual is to work with the district director to establish and maintain the advisory committee. Sustaining a good working relationship with the advisory committee can be difficult, but it is critical to the success of the partnership. Business personnel often are reluctant to participate unless they see specific significant tasks to which they can contribute. In addition to their usual academy role, they can help by inviting academy teachers to visit their companies and work with them for a summer so the teachers can become familiar with the businesses.

It takes time and persistence to develop a mentor program, especially in areas in which there are few large established businesses. Small businesses usually cannot afford to give the mentor support that large companies can. In order to obtain an adequate number of mentors, many small businesses would have to be associated with the partnership. Community service organizations such as Kiwanis and Rotary can sometimes be contacted to supply enough mentors to help a program get started. One school district having difficulty finding enough mentors encouraged its students to become active in community service. The students became so active in charitable events that the local newspaper wrote an article about the program and its need for mentors. Within a short time the academies had all the mentors they needed.

Sometimes individual mentoring relationships do not work out. Some mentors are disconcerted by the students' language, table manners, dress, and inappropriate use of time, or they are disappointed when their mentees do not change overnight. Can academies survive without mentors? Yes, but students would be deprived of important role models, which would have a particularly negative effect on minority students.

Full implementation of the work experience program can be a long and arduous process. A legitimate criticism of the partnership academies is that the program started in Silicon Valley, an area that potentially provides many exciting jobs for students. Moreover, the program provides few guidelines to finding jobs in communities in which there are only small businesses or very few jobs. A large part of this problem is finding a method of involving small businesses in the program. The partnership academies have not solved this problem, which becomes especially acute during an economic downturn.

Another work experience problem is to ensure that businesses do not use the program to replace more expensive adult workers. Companies that have unions are very careful in regard to this issue. Union leaders must be brought into implementation discussions at an early stage. There have been situations in which the program has not been able to place students in businesses with union contracts. Recessions have a serious effect on the trades. When large percentages of their people have no work it is understandable that they are unwilling to hire "pre-apprentices."

Securing an adequate number of good jobs is the most difficult component of the model. The program would be helped immeasurably by a formalized apprenticeship role with businesses, as is found in Germany, where industry finances and carries out technical training. Although most young American adults find gainful employment by their mid twenties, much valuable and productive time is lost when they spend their early work years in marginal jobs. Chapter Six contains further discussion of this and other issues involved in the school-business partnership.

Funding

California has had difficulty starting as many academies as it would like because of recent large deficits in the state budget. Yet the governor's 1992–1993 budget proposal includes funds to continue expanding the program.

Capital costs for the start-up of a career academy can be substantial. Most of these costs are for new equipment or facility modification for the technical lab. After the initial costs there are usually operational costs, such as upkeep, software, and supplies. The other major academy cost is the price that must be paid to reduce the class size and for the additional teacher preparation period. Also the total cost to school districts will be higher because the number of at-risk students is becoming an ever-larger proportion of the school population.

One way to reduce costs would be to provide less release time for teachers after the academy has completed its first three years. A large portion of the curriculum development should be completed by that time. The teachers could maintain their common preparation period but not have an extra released period for the entire year. In addition, retirees could be recruited to fill the business liaison position, and existing work experience coordinators could be assigned to teach employability skills and monitor students on the job. This would be less costly than using regular teachers, and probably just as effective.

As the California Partnership Academy model (like other career academies) evolves to include a more heterogeneous group of students—some clearly college-bound, some at risk of not finishing high school—class sizes also can increase to nearer the school average. This will contribute further to reducing costs.

Guiding Principles

In the struggle to create a new program and overcome obstacles, keeping in mind basic goals or principles helps focus effort and sustain commitment. In our judgment, the four essential principles that sustain career academies are building a sense of community, enhancing teacher professionalism, integrating the curriculum, and facilitating students' transition from school to career. These principles inspire not only the California Partnership Academies but also the NAF and Philadelphia academies.

A Sense of Community

Many parents, students, and teachers find that the feeling of membership in a community is the academy's most powerful feature. Several components of the academy model—the school-within-a-school, small class size, individual attention, guidance/counseling, and parental involvement—directly promote a sense of community among its teachers, students, and parents.

Teachers and counselors in the regular program usually cannot give students much personal support. After teaching 150 or more different students each day, most teachers are too weary and stressed to know when a student is lonely and troubled, let alone to respond to signals for help. Counselors and administrators also lack the time to make a difference in students' lives. Large caseloads leave them barely able to cope with serious absenteeism, substance abuse, and discipline problems, much less with problems of alienation and underachievement.

The closely knit and caring school communities of the academies provide support to students who cannot thrive without a change in their school environment. Students form personal bonds with their school, with one another, with their teachers, and with other positive adult role models. These bonds are created by the school-within-a-school format, and they grow stronger as teachers and students work together for three years. This arrangement permits teachers to give individual attention to students, provide guidance, and work on life as well as academic skills. Many students have spoken about their experience in the academy as that of a large and caring family.

Some educators question the idea of keeping a peer group of at-risk students together for three years, for fear that enrolling them in classes together over such a long period will reinforce poor behavior and habits. However, the experience of academies demonstrates that students can exert a positive influence on one another when they strive for the same goals: graduation, followed by the opportunity for a decent job with good wages or postsecondary education. For many at-risk students, friends are the major reason they go to school. The influence of the friends these students choose is crucial. Students in the academy serve as role models to their fellow students, which helps develop their sense of responsibility. Sophomores and juniors realize what they can achieve when they observe the accomplishments of the seniors. One school administrator noted that some of his students were using the academy at his school as a "safe house to protect them from drug and gang activity."

On many high school campuses different racial and ethnic groups have little social interaction. Students tend to segregate themselves in the classroom, at lunchtime, and during school activities. In contrast, visitors to multiracial academies observe a lack of self-segregation among the students. Being together for three years allows students to know one another as individuals. At one academy, students in the senior English class were discussing what it takes to write a play. The teacher told them that they needed a plot. The students suggested that the play should be about a "bunch of poor dumb whites, Mexicans, and blacks who started in a program together as sophomores, with the different races hating each other on sight, stayed together until their senior year, became best friends, and all went to college!"

Parents are an integral part of the academy community. Evaluations of the academies show that parents are very satisfied with their students' school experience and recognize the value of the sense of community fostered by the academies (Reller, 1984). One parent testified, "I wish the rest of school was like this. It would be wonderful if the rest of the school had teachers like these, who care." Parents feel that the school has given their children a chance for real success in life by promoting personal responsibility and communal support for learning.

Teacher Professionalism

In the academies, management functions that directly affect the classroom are delegated to teachers. Teachers are responsible for developing the integrated curriculum and for ensuring that a group of students graduates. They exercise their professional expertise and judgment to make changes in their class schedules and in the allocation of time. They have control over the curriculum, providing it does not conflict with local and state standards. This authority, combined with the power to recruit and select the students, provides the flexibility needed to operate as an interdisciplinary team that is rarely found in high schools. Empowerment of teachers inspires much of the career academies' success.

Many California Partnership Academies give their teachers a common extra preparation period each day to work together on their additional responsibilities—curriculum development, student recruitment, parental contacts, and planning academy events. The school-within-a-school format and the common free period promote collegiality and encourage working together in a cooperative mode. Team teaching is facilitated, and guest speakers, field trips, and parent conferences are easily arranged. Academy teachers like the common preparation period because it helps break down their traditional isolation.

The autonomy provided by the decentralized management of the school-within-a-school has helped build teacher professionalism and heightened morale. Academy staff gain stature when they serve as disseminators of good practice. They share materials they have used successfully, expertise in using technology to improve instruction, and examples of interdisciplinary curriculum. This leads to more cooperative relationships with their nonacademy colleagues. Teaching materials and techniques that were successfully developed in academies are being used in the regular program at several schools.

The teamwork of the academies teachers generates a strong fellowship. Many find the improved staff relationship to be as important to the success of the program as is the curriculum. One young teacher commented, "Working in a program such as this is what professionals look for when they decide to teach. We work closely with our colleagues and really get to know and like them. Teaching is no longer just an assembly line with students in and students out."

Integrated Curriculum

Academy teachers share the common educational purpose of providing their students with a coherent course of study so that, upon graduation, they can choose either to enter the workplace or to continue their education. This is done by integrating the academies' academic and vocational curricula. As illustrated in Chapter Two, teachers develop thematic units that link their separate classes. Students learn about the same issue in different classes at the same time. Theory is immediately applied.

Teachers find that the integrated curriculum lends itself well to cooperative learning. The school-within-a-school organization provides an atmosphere that encourages collaboration and teamwork among students. Some academies devise entire units to give students a personal understanding of team-work. This experience helps prepare students for the work-place, where teamwork is ubiquitous.

Transition from School to Career

The academy curriculum is influenced by the requirements of adult careers. Schools and businesses work together to help youth make the transition from school to career. Employability skills (promptness, attitude, and dependability) are taught in the classroom. Students get firsthand exposure to career information through field trips, guest speakers, and the mentor program. The jobs they hold during the summer after their junior year and in the spring of their senior year provide a direct transition from the classroom to the workplace.

The mentor program is an important step in the transition to work. Mentors serve as role models, tutors, and confidants. They provide students with career advice, support constructive work habits and attitudes, and can caution students about the effects of delinquency and substance abuse. Disadvantaged students often are most familiar with people who, if gainfully employed, are not in positions of importance. These students do not have the opportunities of middle-class students, who learn from parents and older peers how to get a job, project a positive attitude, and match their talents with the jobs available. They lack the informal network of contacts and knowledge about the world of work that is routine in the middle class.

Many students have very limited ideas about the kinds of work adults do. A young African American engineer took three African American students to a computer graphics firm whose equipment has been used in several recent movies. He showed them some of the equipment and generated some electrifying displays. The students were awestruck. He then told them that only their lack of education would keep them from working at that company or one like it. They came back to class and excitedly told their teachers and classmates that they had seen the future.

The jobs supplied by business to academy students provide the motivation to succeed often lacking in at-risk students. They help keep students in school and provide them with options while they are there. In the academies jobs are provided that reinforce the theme that academics are important for workers to succeed in business. They encourage reluctant students to enter a program that requires extra effort.

Desired Results

The outcome of a student's participation in a career academy is a graduate who is academically and technically proficient, has marketable skills including the capacity for participation in a productive learning community, and is qualified to enroll in postsecondary education. Academy graduates have options that range from enrolling in a community college, a professional institute, or a four-year college; to getting an entry-level job with career prospects; to a combination of further education and employment. Career academies demonstrate that a partnership of caring adults can help young people improve their own chances in life.

SIX

⚔ ○ ⚔

Forging Partnerships
Between Schools and Employers

Career academies depend on a partnership between high schools and employers. Often this is not an easy partnership to form for either schools or businesses. Sometimes teachers and administrators are so apprehensive about approaching employers that they delay until it is too late. Sometimes they just do not know how to go about it.

Reluctance also exists on the business side. Employers may lack the resources to help support an academy, or they may simply see no benefit to themselves in working with a high school. Many employers do not see it as being in their interest to participate in the workforce preparation of students. This is the most difficult obstacle to overcome. However, more employers may be coming to believe that their active participation in training—for students as well as for their existing employees—is essential for their ability to remain competitive, especially against other countries where firms do take more responsibility for creating and renewing the skills and knowledge of the workforce (National Center on Education and the Economy, 1990).

Even when the willingness is there, the partnership requires understanding on both sides. Companies focus on products, schools on students. Companies employ people of

101

all ages; high schools serve a narrow age range of the population. Companies operate on different schedules than schools, on both a daily and a yearly basis. Even the languages of the two sides differ significantly.

Experience with career academies suggests that this model provides a structure for productive partnership. Most academies have established good working relations between schools and employers. Testimony from both sides reflects a growing understanding of each other's point of view and of the necessity for cooperation. The clearly defined roles that academies provide for employers and the clear focus on outcomes and performance are central to this growing sense of teamwork. But the task of building partnerships is rarely easy, and those who would undertake developing an academy must recognize both the importance and the difficulty of this effort.

Employers' Contributions

Too often both business and school staff assume that the most important role for employers is to provide financial support. Or if the company happens to produce something of use to the program, such as computers or software, this may seem to be the best kind of support. While these are certainly welcome if available, they tend to be both difficult for employers to give and less important than other things. There are really two central contributions needed, and they go hand in hand: information and people's time.

What kinds of information does this entail? One goal of career academies is to prepare students for work. To accomplish this, employers must let teachers know what jobs are available and what knowledge, skills, and behavior they require. They must also help develop the program's technical curriculum. Teachers rarely have a very complete conception of this curriculum prior to the academy's creation.

Employers become involved in an academy for a variety of reasons. Discussing these openly from the start will help fulfill employers' purposes as well as the school's. Some businesses want better-prepared entry-level employees and would like to influence the high school curriculum. Some have training programs of their own and are looking for interested and appropriately prepared high school graduates. One employer, when asked why he was interested in participating in an academy, gave a two-word answer: "promotable minorities." He had many Hispanic employees in low-level positions and wanted to move some of them into the management structure of the firm, but he was having trouble finding people with the necessary knowledge and skills. Whatever the employers' objectives, they must be considered in designing the academy.

The other critical resource employers can offer an academy is people's time. It is, of course, only from people that the necessary information discussed above can come. It is also only people who can serve as steering committee members, speakers, field trip hosts, mentors, and work-experience job supervisors. All of these roles are voluntary. Also, allowing employees to work with young people who can so obviously benefit from their attention often builds increased enthusiasm and company loyalty.

Academies are designed to keep employer contributions within reason. Speakers usually need just a class period or two to make their presentations, plus travel time. Mentors are only expected to spend two hours per month with their student, though many contribute extra time on their own. Work supervisors are involved in overseeing the work of employees anyway. The work experience program simply means they are doing it with academy students. This may require more time, but many supervisors react positively to working with a young person, especially if the student is enthusiastic and has been well prepared for the position.

While information and people's time are the two most critical contributions of employers, there are other possibilities. Small amounts of funding, while often more difficult to give, can be very helpful. The same is true of equipment. Sometimes companies have facilities that can be made available for use by students, which is a good way to provide up-to-date training without requiring schools to purchase new

equipment. Sometimes employers also have materials and supplies that can be helpful to academies.

Another kind of useful contribution is the loan of
employees to help with instruction. This can take a number
of forms beyond the standard features of the program (such
as speakers and mentors). For example, one electronics
academy had the loan of a technical instructor for a full year,
someone who was current in his knowledge of the field and
its practices and equipment. More often academies have used
employees who were expert on particular topics to serve as
"guest lecturers," teaching for a few days while their field of
expertise was the topic under consideration.

Still another role employers have played is that of providing staff to help orient teachers to the field, often in summer staff development workshops. In some cases this has
taken the form of providing teachers with summer jobs that
teach them what working in the field is like. This not only
gives teachers welcome work over the summer but provides
invaluable insight they can pass on to their students the next
year. It also provides the employer with interested workers
who may bring useful insights to the job.

Who Should Be Involved and How

Successful academies involve employer representatives from a
variety of levels and at a variety of times in their operations.
Contacts usually begin at a high level. When the high school
and district are deciding whether to form an academy, they
must determine the potential level of employer support. At
this initial stage, contacts usually take place between the highest officials on both sides: the district superintendent or assistant superintendent and high school principal on one side,
and either the chief executive officer or someone close to him
or her on the other. Initial interest and commitment should
come from the top. Once this is determined, the details can be
worked out at lower levels.

There are several reasons for this. One is that high-
level officials on both sides are usually visionary enough to

see the value of the partnership they are forming and to avoid getting sidetracked by the possible difficulties of implementation. Another reason is that these officials can indicate their commitment to those below them in a way that will result in the necessary follow-up activity. CEOs have lines of command through which they can delegate responsibilities, as do superintendents and principals. While academies usually do not require substantial time or involvement from this top level, they do need an initial investment if they are to be successful.

Once initial interest and commitment are established at a high level on both sides, responsibility for follow-up usually passes to lower levels. On the employer side, often someone from the human resources or community affairs division assumes this responsibility. On the school side, usually a district administrator of special programs, high school curriculum director, or vocational education director takes over. The responsible individuals should possess enough authority to be able to make the commitments necessary for the operation of the program.

There is no substitute for good organization in coordinating employer involvement. There needs to be someone in charge at the school or district who can serve as a central point of contact. It is helpful if the same is true with each employer, especially if the firm is large. The school contact must have his or her own telephone that can be used throughout the day. One of the biggest frustrations of employers in working with schools is being unable to reach a teacher or administrator. Most academies have telephones installed in the classroom of the lead teacher, and students come to expect this and learn how to answer it professionally when needed.

It is also usually necessary to survey companies for staff interest in participating in various components of the academy. This is accomplished in many ways: through flyers, announcements at staff meetings, electronic mail, and word of mouth. Sign-up sheets can be used to follow up. Since employers are often approached by many worthy causes, it is important to use methods that are acceptable to the company. If several academies are operating in the same geographical area, it is useful for them to make their approaches in common.

One example of this unified approach involves several academies located near the original academies on the San Francisco Peninsula that decided to band together to approach companies, calling themselves the Bay Area Partnership Academies. The purpose was to approach companies just once for their combined needs. An "Academy Resource Application" form was developed, listing a variety of activities employees might select. This enabled the academies to develop a resource pool from which they all could draw.

An example of even broader collaboration exists among the Philadelphia academies. As discussed in Chapter Three, the sixteen individual academies throughout that district have merged under one structure called the Philadelphia High School Academies, Inc. (PHSA). PHSA has a board of directors that includes leaders from business, labor, and the school district. PHSA receives most of its support from the more than thirty-five companies involved with academies in Philadelphia, and it employs three full-time staff members to coordinate resource development and job placements among these companies. Among the participating employers are some of the largest corporations in Philadelphia, as well as numerous small and midsize businesses. By coordinating connections with employers throughout the city, PHSA can eliminate redundant approaches to companies, ensure that each academy receives what it most needs, and balance resources fairly across the sixteen programs.

How Many Employers and When

How many employers are needed depends on the type of academy and the size of the employers. One of the academies in California is associated with Gottschalks, a large department store chain. In this case, since the training is directly related to working in the chain's stores and there are ample resources from this one source, only the one employer is involved. In a similar case, an academy is associated with

Safeway, a large supermarket grocery chain. More typically an academy works best if several employers are involved to share the required efforts. where there are no large employers available, there may need to be many small ones.

Perhaps the best examples of employer involvement come from some of the older and better-established academies in California. For example, the two programs on which the model is based, the computer and electronics academies in the Sequoia district, have involved a number of large Silicon Valley companies, including such giants as Hewlett-Packard, Lockheed, Tandem, Xerox, and IBM. The health academy at Oakland Technical High School has involved several hospitals, as well as a school of nursing and a number of private practitioners. In contrast, two agribusiness academies located in small rural communities in the Central Valley have pieced together a mixture of an occasional large firm (for example, the poultry producer Foster Farms) and many small business representatives whose companies support agriculture in some way.

The criterion for determining how many companies to involve is whether there is a large enough employee base to support the various program activities. For example, during the junior year there must be enough employees to provide a mentor for each student, usually around forty. That summer there have to be enough work experience positions so that most of the junior class can have paid jobs (except students who need to attend summer school to make up credits). Large companies can usually supply many of these, small ones only one or two.

The three-year progression of the academy is designed to allow the gradual development of employer involvement. The initial top-level commitments should result in members for the steering committee to help plan and guide the program. These officials meet regularly, usually quarterly, to set program policy and guide important decisions. This body is critical during the planning phase and continues its role as the program moves through the various stages of implementation. Specifically, the steering committee

- Establishes a working task force that brings together teachers and employers' representatives to define what students should know and be able to do when they leave the academy and to help identify the curriculum necessary to achieve these objectives
- Identifies the resources needed from employers to operate the program, such as speakers, field trip sites, and mentors, and determines how to obtain these for the program
- Provides a joint education and employer perspective in making decisions about how the program will be structured and operated
- Serves as a point of contact to the broader employer community, informing it about the program and developing wider support

During the first program year speakers and field trips are the main avenue of employer involvement. Usually there are more speakers than field trips, sometimes as many as one a week. Their purpose is to motivate and inform students, giving them examples of successes in the field and information about the variety of career possibilities. Field trips usually take place once every few weeks. Their purpose is to provide a firsthand look at various workplaces and at companies in the local geographical region that hire people with the kinds of preparation the academy provides.

Both speakers and field trip hosts can be from almost any level of the company, assuming they represent job levels the students might aim for and have enough knowledge to describe the company and its positions. Some of the best speakers are those who began at low levels and worked their way up, as they understand the students' backgrounds as well as the value of hard work and commitment. Often field trips include several different hosts, who explain various aspects of the company and its products. Sometimes lunches are provided, a perk that students appreciate.

Generally neither speakers nor field trips are difficult to arrange. Often employers offer these to schools on a regular basis, even without an academy. However, the mentor program that begins in the junior year requires a more substantial commitment—namely, the willingness of employees to volunteer to work with students on a one-on-one basis. Thus it is important during the planning period and the first program year to build employer support within companies that will make it possible to secure the mentors when needed.

This is even more true of the work experience component. Employers often hire academy students into positions to which they would otherwise have little access. While some companies have summer-hire programs for young people many do not. Thus summer jobs may have to be arranged as a new program at the place of work, which requires considerable preparation and planning. The senior-year part-time afternoon jobs may be even more difficult for employers, who may lack part-time positions as a normal part of their staffing system. Another factor affecting the supply of positions is the state of the economy. During recessions such jobs are likely to be even more difficult to supply. The value of the program and the commitment of the employers must be established during the planning phase and the first year or two of operation to overcome such difficulties when they arise.

The Mentor Program

The original Peninsula Academies in California developed a "Mentor Handbook," with sections that cover the key features of the program. Many of the newer academies have adapted this to their own uses. This handbook includes

- An explanation of the nature and purpose of the academies
- A description of what roles a mentor plays
- A list of typical mentor activities
- Sketches and job positions of some typical mentors
- A description of how mentors are matched with students
- A registration form and contacts for further information

Mentors come from all levels and roles within companies, from high-level managers to line workers. Their common denominator is a willingness to work with students who may not be performing particularly well in school (although by the junior year, when this part of the program operates, most have begun to improve) but are interested in the field of training. They must also be able to give students an overview of the jobs available in the field and the training required to reach various levels. And they must be willing to spend at least two hours per month with the student. Typical student/ mentor activities include:

- Touring the mentor's company, introducing the student to co-workers, and showing him or her typical work areas and jobs
- Touring the student's school and learning about the academy
- Inviting the student to special company activities, such as presentations, picnics, and sports activities
- Getting together for lunch
- Discussing books on technical information and topics of interest
- Discussing potential careers in the student's field of training
- Working on a project together, such as assembling a kit or developing a computer program
- Visiting another site of interest, such as another company, a jobs fair, or a technical show
- Working on a subject the student is finding difficult
- Discussing basic features of holding a job, such as punctuality, reliability, dress, and speech
- Preparing students for interviews for summer jobs; maintaining contact over the summer to discuss problems that may arise on the job
- Discussing plans for college

The process of identifying mentors and matching them to students begins in the spring prior to the school year in which they will serve and continues over the summer and into the fall. Mentors are carefully matched to students on the basis of interests and, where possible, gender and ethnicity. Usually the mentors and students meet each other at the school at an arranged "mentor meeting" organized by the teachers early in the fall semester. Mentors contact the students' parents and keep them informed of their activities. The mentor activities typically begin in October and last through the rest of the school year.

Usually the main employer contact, typically a member of the steering committee, identifies someone within the company to serve as a "mentor coordinator" for that employer. This person distributes information about the program throughout the company and handles inquiries. Those employees who want to participate are asked to complete a registration form that provides information on their job and interests that can be used in matching them to students.

Employees who sign up to be mentors attend an orientation workshop that gives them details on the program and guidance in how to be an effective mentor. This workshop is usually held at either the district's meeting rooms or one of the participating employer's facilities shortly before the matchup with students. Teachers and administrators review the roles and responsibilities of a mentor and discuss useful activities. A typical student profile is also presented, and often one or more students attend to help answer questions. If the program is not in its first year, past mentors also attend to describe their experiences.

Operating a successful mentor program involves handling many details. Not all matchups work, and some adjustments usually have to be made. Sometimes not enough mentors volunteer, and so two students are matched to each mentor. This arrangement often has the advantage of easing the initial period of getting acquainted, with three people to interact, but it may result in less attention per student over time. There are insurance implications to be examined in conducting mentor activities, such as in transporting students to activities. Also parents must be informed of the program, and mentors and parents should have some contact before activities begin, by telephone if not in person. The program runs more smoothly if there are occasional academy-wide mentor activities, so that the burden of arranging such activities is not left entirely to individual mentor/student pairs.

While managing such details takes a lot of work, students appreciate the results. Following are examples of what students have had to say about their mentor experiences:

> I feel that my mentor is one of the most outstanding mentors who has ever been involved with the academies. He is the kind of person who cares about the minds of the young people of today. My mentor is always there when I have a problem that either involves school or something personal. He will always take time to help me or give his advice to me.

> My mentor was the person who convinced me to keep furthering my education. For example, he was the one who enrolled me in the PSAT test last fall, and he also bought me the SAT preparation book. He is also the one who pushes me to reach for my goals in life. For example, he and I sometimes talk about my future and my schooling and how I can pursue a career in industry. He has taken me to industry and let me get the feeling of the business world.

Work Experience

As with the mentor program, the Peninsula Academies developed a "Work Experience Handbook" to provide an overview of this feature of the program to students and employers. This handbook covers

- The nature and purpose of the academies
- What "work experience" means
- Typical jobs into which students are placed
- How the program is structured

- How students are evaluated
- How students and employers can participate

The California Partnership Academy model calls for work experience to occur at two points in the academy program: during the summer following the junior year and during the afternoons of the last semester of the senior year. In actual practice, where positions are available, some academies place students in jobs at the end of their sophomore year also (if the students are deemed ready), and some seniors have part-time jobs in the fall as well as the spring semester.

These jobs give students practical, on-the-job experience so they can test and improve their skills in real work settings. Where possible, these experiences include a variety of jobs, so that students are exposed to a range of possibilities in their field of training. These are paid jobs in which students are expected to produce results just as regular employees do. Salaries are determined on a basis consistent with the employer's practices and policies. Each student is assigned a work supervisor who knows of the academy and can guide the student through the experience.

The hiring procedure begins with the employer providing the academies with information on the number and types of positions it has available. For the summer jobs, this occurs in the spring, usually during April. The academy staff then matches appropriate students with the available jobs. Students complete applications, provide resumes, and attend interviews as requested. The employer can set up interviews for students through the work experience coordinator. Only those students who have earned enough credits to be on target for graduation are eligible to work, and then only if the academy teachers deem them ready. About three-fourths of a class typically qualifies.

Once interviews are completed, the employer makes a hiring decision and informs both the student or students and the work experience coordinator. Every attempt is made to be responsive to individual company needs and to provide the best possible candidate for each position. There is no obligation for a company to hire any particular student or to commit to hiring a specific number of students. Nor is there any obligation on the company's part to continue students' employment beyond the end of the summer or semester.

Although there has been much preparation for this work experience, often students are nervous about it. To prepare them, the program offers classes on what to expect and how to prepare for the job. Representatives of employers hiring the students are asked to attend and answer questions such as:

- How should I dress?
- What is the job schedule? How many hours per day and days per week will I work? Will I have to work overtime?
- How do I learn what all my job responsibilities are?
- How do I ask for a day off if I need to take one?
- How is my salary determined? What is taken out of it?
- How will I know where to go the first day?
- Will I receive training about what I am supposed to do?
- What happens if I am late?
- Am I required to do a certain amount of work each day?
- What should I do if something goes wrong?
- How will our co-workers regard us?

If the students are hired, as most are, their first few days on the job typically are challenging. Students must learn not only the details of their jobs but often all the facets of being employed, including being on time, getting along with co-workers, pay schedules and procedures, and so on. According to their teachers, most students emerge from this experience with a much fuller sense of what a job entails and with far greater confidence about their ability to succeed in one. The period between the spring of the junior year and the fall of the senior year marks a dramatic increase in self-esteem for many academy students.

A program representative from the school visits each student and supervisor after the job begins to see that things are going well. If there are problems, they are addressed;

employment can be terminated at any time. In many cases students earn credits as well as pay, which requires some classwork to be associated with the work experience. At the end of the summer or semester, work supervisors complete evaluations of the students, rating them on such matters as

- Accuracy of work
- Care of working area
- Use of equipment and materials
- Speed in performing duties
- Use of working time
- Job learning and application
- Reliability
- Initiative
- Attendance
- Attitude toward co-workers
- Attitude toward superiors
- Personal appearance

Typical ratings have been quite good, averaging about four on a five-point scale. Many supervisors also respond with written comments, often expressing their satisfaction with the work of the academy students. Here are two examples:

I am always pleased to laud high individual performance. For that reason it gives me a great deal of pleasure to acknowledge the talent and ability of this student. . . . [T]he jobs he handled for us were not menial tasks. Computer input, tracking data, gathering statistics, accounting, and preparing reports are all essential to our daily operation. He has been exposed to all of these facets and willingly accepted the responsibilities. . . . His attitude and self-conduct are enduring assets.

Brian's part-time employment included doing cables and some mechanical assembly. He learned fast, did neat and accurate work. He managed his time honestly and could be depended on to finish his assignment on time. He contributed in many ways to our SID 2110 line. He was well liked in our department, and we will miss him.

There is a good deal of debate in the country currently about how much and what types of work experience are ideal. Many experts agree that work experience is most effective if it is tied to courses and training the student takes in school, and if it is carefully monitored and supervised so as to be a useful experience to the student. It also seems to be best if the work is in a position that can lead to fulfilling career possibilities, as opposed to "dead-end jobs." Some research suggests that, at least during the school year, work should not exceed fifteen to twenty hours per week (Steinberg, 1989) and that it should be seen as subservient to school, not the other way around. Adolescents should be discouraged from placing "the short-term goal of earning and spending money above the long-term goal of investing in educational activities likely to contribute to their development into a skilled and innovative worker" (Task Force on Youth Employment, Wisconsin Department of Public Instruction, 1990, p. 21). The academy work experience meets all these criteria.

Teachers report substantial gains in student self-esteem following their work experience. Seniors return in the fall buoyed by their success and able to place their courses and training in a real work context. They become a valuable source of information to the next class and serve as tutors in helping the juniors prepare for their placements. They also often provide worthwhile feedback to teachers concerning current technology and practices in the workplace.

There seem to be several reasons why the work experience proves so valuable. Part of the value seems to derive from simply being paid for one's time. Society also accords a certain status to those who are employed, and students gain a new respect in the eyes of their parents and friends. The logs students keep reveal many other positive features as well. Getting to know co-workers and feeling comfortable around them is important. Realizing that they are capable of performing work of genuine use to a company is rewarding. Learning the simple responsibilities of being at work every day, ready to perform at their best, contributes to their self-confidence. By observing co-workers students also see the value of additional education and its effect on job and income levels. Many return from their work experience determined to go on for postsecondary education, and with their ambitions considerably heightened. This may be the most valuable aspect of the experience.

Career Academies and Youth Apprenticeships

While much detail has been presented here on how to implement the various features of an academy school-business partnership, it all depends on establishing such a partnership in the first place. If that happens, the rest will follow. And the critical step in establishing that partnership is educating the leaders on both sides on their joint responsibility for better workforce preparation.

There are many national agencies and commissions focused on this need. One such is the Council of Chief State School Officers, an organization of state superintendents of schools. In the 1991–92 school year their focus of activity was on school-to-work transition in general and on "youth apprenticeships" in particular. Several states are working currently to explore such possibilities. The career academy model offers a foundation on which to build. In the words of one expert exploring workable models for youth apprenticeship, "Academies . . . are perhaps the closest thing to youth apprenticeship that currently exists in the United States" (Kazis, 1991, p. 5).

SEVEN

--≒ ○ ⊨--

Building on Local Strengths:
Examples from Four Districts

Although all California Partnership Academies spring from
the same legislated model, they are not identical clones. The
model is complex, and replication is subject to many contin-
gencies, which the preceding two chapters have tried to help
readers anticipate.

In the process of implementation, local personalities,
history, and opportunities cause new programs to grow in
different directions. This chapter describes four districts in
which particular elements of the academy model are especially
well developed: integrated curriculum in the Sequoia district;
high-quality summer jobs in Oakland; East San Jose's strong
partnership with business; and Pasadena's use of academies
in the center of a curricular sequence from seventh grade to
four-year college. These descriptions may suggest how other
districts can build on their own local strengths.

Sequoia Union High School District

In 1988 the U.S. Department of Education (USDE) announced
that it would fund ten national demonstration sites for replication of successful dropout prevention programs through
the use of vocational education (Hayward, Tallmadge, and

Leu, 1991). Sequoia Union High School District won a grant to replicate the California Partnership Academies program at two high schools, Carlmont and Woodside, which did not yet have academies (the other two high schools, Sequoia and Menlo-Atherton, are the sites of the original Peninsula Academies). The demonstration program is described here to highlight the process of developing an integrated curriculum for a partnership academy.

Planning the New Curriculum

Marilyn Raby, who had been the district director of the Peninsula Academies, wrote the grant proposal and became district director of the new academies. Business technology, emphasizing the use of computers, was chosen as the career focus. It is a field that has many job opportunities for students in the local area and that can lead to careers with upward mobility for students who graduate from the program. Sequoia district's previous involvement in adopt-a-school-programs was the determining factor in the selection of this vocational area for the new academies. IBM and Hotel Sofitel had adopted Carlmont High, and Stanford Shopping Center, a large and successful complex on the edge of Stanford University's campus, had adopted Woodside High. Consequently, many different jobs and considerable technical assistance were available to help set up a business technology academy.

The business department chairpersons at the two high schools volunteered to become chairpersons of the two academies. They worked with the principals and the district academies director to decide which teachers to recruit. Attracting highly qualified staff was made easier by the positive reputation of the academies at the district's other two high schools.

The major developmental task was to create a curriculum that would integrate computer skills for business with the core academic courses: English, social studies, and mathematics. The curriculum was to be built around analysis and solution of problems: identifying the problem, analyzing available resources and tools, and working out a step-by-step solution. This process was to be applied at all levels, from learning English, math, and social studies, to dealing with job relationships, to planning a career. The intent was to prepare the students to succeed in postsecondary education and to advance quickly beyond entry-level jobs.

The USDE grant provided funds for a planning period to develop the new curriculum. Eight teachers spent three weeks during the summer designing the integrated curriculum. They used part of this time for an intensive period of brainstorming to select organizing themes for the integrated units. The use of themes creates a contextual relationship between the academic and vocational courses by allowing students to look at a topic from several different perspectives. The teachers decided that each discipline also must stand as a separate subject to provide an opportunity for students having trouble with basic concepts or skills to receive extra help.

Course content was formulated by examining curriculum outlines and materials already used in Sequoia and other districts. The teachers used the established state and district curriculum frameworks as guides to sequence and to coordinate the content in the academic and vocational/technical courses. This ensured that the coursework provided students with the information and skills required by the state subject matter frameworks, by the district and state competency tests, and for admission to college. It also reduced the possible difficulty a student might have in transferring from the academy back to the regular school program or to another school.

The USDE grant also provided funds to purchase computer equipment for the business technology laboratories at each school. Each lab was equipped with twenty-six IBM PS/2 Model 30 computers for the students and an IBM PS/2 model 55 computer for the teachers. Funding for a fileserver and to link all the computers at each site in a network was obtained through an award from IBM's California Education Partnership Joint Development Project. IBM provided two weeks of training for teachers, introducing them to word processing, data base, spreadsheet, desktop publishing, and multimedia applications; teacher productivity tools; and subject matter–specific software. This training made it possible to use the computer laboratory to support the integrated curriculum.

Every student has access to a personal computer for at least one period each day. The computers are used to present the coursework in business technology and some academic lessons. Students experiment in the computer labs during their free time. Visitors are often impressed by students' reluctance to leave when the bells ring for class and even for lunch. Substitute teachers have sometimes been asked by students by leave them alone so they can continue their work without interference.

Grade 10

The first-year curriculum aims to get students on track for graduation by bringing them up to grade level in reading, writing, and mathematics. Students take a full year of English, social science (Western Civilization), mathematics, and business technology in the academies. They also take non-academy classes in physical education and science.

The whole-language concept is used in English to integrate reading, writing, listening, and speaking skills. The tenth-grade course begins with a unit on goal setting, time management, study habits, test preparation, and information search techniques. For example, since inquiry skills are emphasized, tenth-grade students go on a field trip to the city library. They divide into teams of three and seek answers to several pages of questions that expose them to the library's variety of materials and services. Students work cooperatively, and each member of a team receives the same grade. For most of the students this is their first introduction to the many services available in a city library.

Emphasis on study skills continues throughout the year and is applied to composition, grammar, vocabulary, and literature. Writing receives the highest priority. Students learn that writing is an essential means of communication in the business world. Writing is always done for a purpose that is meaningful to students. A variety of techniques are used: journals, proofreading, business writing (resumes, letters, and memos), and the publication of an academy newsletter. Students read technical manuals and write instructions to describe such work-related processes as how to replace an ink cartridge on a printer. Vocabulary lessons include computer terminology and the language of business.

Social studies in grade 10 is a year-long course in Western civilization designed to give academy students a multicultural overview. It includes the contributions of African, Asian, European, and Latin American people to social and political institutions, ethical and religious ideas, and other cultural attainments. The course is designed to promote cultural literacy and give the students an understanding of what humans have accomplished throughout history. Appropriate works of literature and the humanities enrich each unit.

The few entering students who have the necessary mathematical background and skills enroll in Algebra I. Most enroll in a transitional mathematics course developed at the University of Chicago. It is designed for students who are proficient at whole-number arithmetic but who have weaknesses in areas such as fractions, decimals, and percentages. The course emphasizes fundamental skills and concepts required for a technological society. Mathematical ideas are studied through applications and practical problems. The course content includes measurement, geometry, statistics, probability, logic, and algebra. Reading and problem solving are stressed. The use of calculators is routine because their efficiency in doing computations allows students to spend more time on the important aspects of problem solving. Students are expected to do homework every night and to take algebra the next year. Students comment that the math is hard but interesting. Wherever possible the history of major ideas and recent developments in mathematics and their application is correlated with coursework in Western Civilization.

The business technology course provides instruction in using computer keyboards and word processors, setting up and using data bases for business computations, and communicating via electronic mail over local networks. Employability skills and an orientation to careers in business technology are included. Students spend approximately four class hours a week in lectures, demonstrations, exercises, and quizzes on business technology, and one class hour a week in career exploration. Each student keeps a folder containing a list of unit objectives, class notes, handouts, assignments, projects, quizzes, and tests.

Computer coursework in business technology is coordinated with English, social studies, and math from the very beginning. English compositions are written using word processor, speller, and grammar-checker software. In the Western civilization course students use the computer to make timelines and do simulation exercises in geography. Computers also are an integral part of the math course. Critical thinking is stimulated by such problems as, "If you have only one square root to calculate, a calculator is faster than a computer. If you have to calculate the square roots of whole numbers from 1 to 1,000, a computer is faster. Since you have both a calculator and a computer, how many square roots would you have to calculate before you would use your computer, and why?"

Participating businesses play an important role in the tenth-grade curriculum. Students take field trips to local businesses, where they are introduced to the workplace. Motivation to study is provided by Hotel Sofitel's monthly award program. The four or five students whom the teachers choose as the most improved each month in such areas as attendance and classwork are invited, with their teachers, to have lunch in the hotel's elegant dining room. These visits have sparked a poignant interest in grooming and behavior among the students. One boy felt he should not go because he had never owned a pair of "hard" shoes. Several students asked their English teacher to get them some books on etiquette so they would not be embarrassed by their limited knowledge of table manners.

Grade 11

The goals of the eleventh-grade curriculum are to broaden and deepen students' academic learning and to prepare them for their first jobs in business. Elements of business communication (for example, selecting letter formats and styles, developing shell documents) are introduced and continue throughout the English sequence. Twentieth-century America is the theme that ties together mathematics, English, U.S. history, and computer skills. For example, the U.S. history course, using a text with a strong multicultural emphasis, raises many questions about the Great Depression of the 1930s. What were its causes? How did the government respond? What were the effects on rural and urban families, Mexican Americans, women, and sharecroppers? What was the role of radio and movies? In English students read *The Grapes of Wrath*. They write timed responses on programs they would have proposed to help the nation, take oral histories from older members of their families, and make presentations on the problems their grandparents faced during the period. This integrated approach helps bring the material to life.

Eleventh-grade students use an algebra text that covers a wider scope than in the traditional algebra course. It includes work on statistics, probability, and geometry, and it continues the work with calculators and computers. Mathematics is integrated with history and computers through assignments such as this: Select five common job titles, find the yearly wage for each job in 1930, then compute the average yearly wage for all five jobs. Repeat this process for the same jobs using wages in 1990. Compute one job's percentage of the average wage of all five jobs in 1930. Repeat this process for the same job in 1990. Find the growth (decline) of relative wages for this job. Then choose appropriate software to display the findings graphically. In this manner students describe historical change quantitatively, using computers.

Students begin to use multimedia software in the computer lab. They are introduced to desktop publishing and start producing large documents, such as a newsletter. There is an emphasis on workplace literacy, diagnosing and solving problems, and working productively in groups. Students update their résumés and practice interviewing techniques for their summer jobs. They continue to have guest speakers from industry who, among other things, critique them on their interviewing skills.

During the spring participating businesses interview students for summer jobs. Students are not promised jobs. They are promised interviews if they are on track for graduation and are recommended by all their academy teachers. Students not on track for graduation must attend summer school. In 1991 80 percent of the first class of students was hired. Evaluations by their job supervisors averaged above three on a four-point scale.

Grade 12

In twelfth grade the English, social studies, and computer courses are integrated around themes of economics, ethics, and personal success. Focusing on values and individual growth confronts students with ideas of democracy, responsibility, and freedom. In social studies, one semester each of economics and American government is required. English students read *Hamlet* and current biographies such as *Iacocca*. In English and in the business technology course students work on formal presentations. For example, student teams present a new product to their classmates. They prepare visuals, develop a brochure, anticipate and prepare for questions, and give the actual presentation. Thoroughness of preparation, presentation skills, responsibility, and diligence are emphasized.

Academy students must complete at least two years of mathematics, including algebra. Students who have shown the ability and interest take geometry and sometimes advanced algebra in non-academy classes. Most students complete the mathematics portion of the academy program before twelfth grade, but mathematics continues to be integrated into social studies and business technology. Students use estimation and approximation techniques and construct graphs for displaying statistical data in their government and economics classes.

In the twelfth-grade career component, students begin an intensive exploration of options beyond high school. They take field trips to the local community college and to the University of California, Berkeley, or Stanford University. They survey careers, research a company, and write résumés, job applications, and applications to state and community colleges. In the second semester students are scheduled for half-day work experience with a participating company. Some of these positions phase into regular jobs for students upon graduation.

Instructional Formats

A variety of formats and strategies are used to build academic competence. These include small-group instruction, small class size, cooperative learning, tutoring, and bilingual support when needed. Individualized attention and small-group instruction help teachers become familiar with their students' academic strengths and weaknesses. Small class size allows a teacher to interact with fewer students in greater depth. It also helps develop a sense of community among the students and teachers. In English it allows teachers to assign, discuss, and grade more writing assignments. Smaller class size allows teachers to get to know and care about the students. One teacher remarked, "I know my students so well that I don't have to accept anything but improvement from them, because I know what they can do."

Cooperative learning simulates experience in the business world. Students learn to solve problems by collaborating to organize their work and collect data. They discover how much and what kind of effort is necessary to complete various tasks. They also learn effective interpersonal interactions needed to work together as a team on a project. The school-within-a-school format supports cooperative learning. Extensive use of computers also stimulates student collaboration. Students sit closer to one another and share more ideas around a computer than in regular classes.

Students who enter the program with academic skill deficiencies need special tutoring. This happens in several ways. Most commonly, classroom teachers and instructional aides provide it during lunchtime and after school. Students tutor each other informally as a matter of course. Some adult mentors tutor their protègès. In addition there are special programs at the high schools for all students who have basic skills deficiencies or who require special help to enter college.

English is the second language for approximately one of every three students in the business technology academies. Extra support is provided for these students through the use of sheltered English, which combines basic English language development with specialized content instruction in English. Each academy has a bilingual teacher or instructional aide to offer help in the students' primary language. Adequate resources for limited-English-proficient students is a serious and growing problem at both high schools due to the recent influx of immigrants from Latin America and Southeast Asia.

Student Assessment

Teachers' evaluations of students are kept positive. Academy teachers try to build students' self-esteem, not destroy it. Harsh comments in red ink are avoided. Computers are helpful because they can point out errors in a nonjudgmental fashion. Each student builds a cumulative portfolio that contains a range of work, including the student's business card; examples of business communications, letters, and memos; and examples of the creative use of desktop publishing, data bases and spreadsheets. The portfolios also include any awards the students may have earned, job evaluations, résumés and references, and other personal material they would like to add, such as lists of books they have read or trips they have taken. Upon graduation, in addition to a high school diploma, each student receives a certificate of completion that lists the skills and knowledge he or she has mastered in computers and business technology.

Teachers have noticed a definite change both in mastery of subject matter and in students' attitudes between the sophomore and senior years, a change that involves more than simple maturation. Academy students find the integrated curriculum interesting—an antidote to their usual boredom with academic work. As a result, they show a marked improvement in their grades though the courses are more demanding. One student commented, "In this program teachers show you what you can be if you really try." Students who were antagonistic and uninterested before they entered the program become more motivated, cooperative, and ambitious. They see a purpose to their school courses and understand the importance of completing assignments. Their attendance improves dramatically, as does their self-esteem.

Almost all seniors plan some form of postsecondary education. The business technology academies are demonstrating that intervention in grades 10 through 12 is not too late for at-risk youth. As one student put it, "Doing all that hard work made me feel so important, so high up there." Student athletes in the program have sailed through the new and tougher National Collegiate Athletic Association (NCAA) academic requirements. Their coaches have been astonished not only by their SAT scores but also by the athletes' intense pride in their accomplishment.

Oakland

The Oakland Academies are notable because they show how California Partnership Academies can flourish in a big-city setting. Oakland is a city of approximately 350,000, located across the bay from San Francisco, with a sizable population of African Americans and growing populations of Hispanics and Asians. The Oakland economy is not as oriented toward high technology as is that of the Silicon Valley. Health is a major industry, with several large hospitals in the area. The first Oakland Academy focused on careers in health.

Oakland Technical High School, where the health academy is located, is approximately 75 percent African American and 20 percent Asian. The health academy was one of the programs to receive a grant in the first round of state replications in the fall of 1985. It proved to be very successful, even though operating in a difficult inner-city environment.

This experience prompted the district to use the academy model as the basis for its magnet programs in all six of the city's high schools and to appoint a district director for the programs. Accordingly, as of 1991 there were five other academies operating in Oakland, focusing on media, pre-engineering, business, computer technology, and the performing arts. A law and government academy and a visual arts academy were also starting up.

The Health Academy

The health academy enjoyed strong support from within the Oakland district. The key initiator was the lead teacher, who taught English in the program and organized many of the other activities. Extremely hard working and unusually knowledgeable, she was effective in working with both employers and students. Her principal was also sold on the academy approach and provided much support. They were able to assemble a strong team of teachers as well. More recently, the district director of academies has provided support from that level.

Development of the health academy curriculum required extensive efforts over several years, resulting in a challenging series of courses integrated with practical experience and career development. In science, for example, sophomores take biology, juniors physiology, and seniors chemistry. English is taught at all three grade levels. Other courses include math, computers, personal health, and health occupations. Much of the Oakland Tech health academy curriculum has now been compiled into a binder that makes it available to new academies beginning in this field.

The support provided initially to the health academy and since that time extended increasingly to the others has been impressive. In 1991 Oakland had three state partnership academy grants, as many as any other district in the state. For the past several years the health academy has also enjoyed a grant from another state program, the California Academic Partnership (CAP) program, which roughly doubles its funding. For the 1990–91 and 1991–92 school years the city itself invested $1.2 million dollars from its redevelopment funds in several of Oakland's academies, including the health academy.

The private sector has also contributed substantially. Kaiser Permanente, the largest health maintenance organization in northern California, provides support to the health academy from several of its facilities, from both management and labor staff. Children's Hospital is also supportive. Samuel Merritt College of Nursing provides curriculum development help, has its students serve as tutors to academy students, and allows students and staff in the program to attend professional meetings. Private doctors and dentists hire students as well. An evaluation conducted during the 1987–88 school year found that local employers' representatives had spent more than one thousand days helping the health academy in various ways: serving on the advisory committee, helping plan and evaluate the program, speaking to groups of students, organizing and leading field trips, serving as mentors, arranging job placements, and supervising students on the job.

The Oakland Tech health academy was evaluated from the fall of 1985 through June 1988 (Dayton, Weisberg, and Stern, 1989) as part of the statewide assessment of the initial ten academy replications described in Chapter Four. Data were collected on school performance for both the academy students and a matched group of comparison students. The data from the three years showed that health academy students outperformed their comparison group counterparts on twenty-one of twenty-five statistical tests, fifteen of which were statistically significant. Academy students showed better attendance, credits, and grade point averages; fewer courses failed; and a lower probability of dropping out.

In addition, a separate evaluation of the health academy (along with the media academy at Fremont High School in Oakland) was conducted by the Far West Laboratory for Educational Research and Development (Guthrie, Guthrie, and van Heusden, 1990). A particular strength of this evaluation was a series of in-depth interviews with students. The authors found improvement in academy students' attitudes toward school, as well as in standardized test scores, grades, and preparation for college. They concluded, "The majority of students served by the two academies came from communities populated by the 'truly disadvantaged,' where poverty and crime were common. In this context, getting a good education is often impossible. . . . High school academies like those in Oakland may be the key to breaking the vicious cycle. Even though the two academies in the Oakland Unified School District are not without problems in actual implementation, and even though the academies did not succeed fully in graduating all their students, both the media and the health academies, nevertheless, have accomplished the nearly impossible with a significant number of urban at-risk youth. The interviews conducted with the graduating class in both academies revealed a group of confident, interested, and ambitious young adults" (pp. 24–25).

Other Academies in Oakland

The media academy at John C. Fremont High School was initiated a year after the health academy. Like the health academy, it benefited from the unusual energy and talent of a teacher who took on the responsibility of acting as program director. At the media academy it was the journalism teacher who played this role. This teacher has a strong commitment to empowering students. He has involved them not only in publishing the school newspaper but also in creating a newspaper in Spanish and English for the largely Hispanic community around the high school. Within the academy he has worked closely with an English teacher to create a coherent, integrated curriculum. A broadcast teacher and a math instructor are also part of the team. The academy advisory committee includes local leaders in newspaper publishing, television, and radio. In addition to the positive evaluation by Far West Laboratory summarized above, the media academy also was featured in a book describing exemplary programs for high-risk students (Wehlage and others, 1989).

In 1987 another academy started at Oakland Technical

High School, in pre-engineering. The nucleus of the pre-engineering academy is a partnership between a physics teacher and an instructor in drafting and geometry. These two created a course sequence that leads students from drafting and engineering graphics through descriptive geometry and on into the study of physics. Students build on their proficiency in graphical analysis to understand concepts in statistics, calculus, and Newtonian dynamics. The approach is problem focused: "They learn physics by doing engineering," in the physics teacher's formulation. One stated goal of the advanced physics course is for students to "use basic mathematical reasoning—arithmetic, algebra, geometry, trigonometry, or calculus, where appropriate—in a physical situation or problem." This approach treats various forms of mathematics as problem-solving tools and tries to avoid reducing math to a useless collection of disconnected formulas and procedures. In addition to this tightly conceived sequence in drafting, math, and physics, the pre-engineering academy curriculum also includes courses in history, literature, and world cultures.

As of 1991 Oakland was sponsoring five more academies in addition to those in health, media, and pre-engineering. At McClymonds High School a business academy began in 1986; this was the same year the media academy started at Fremont, but the business academy took longer to get organized. Turnover of principals was one reason for the slow progress. Lack of consistent support from the principal's office delayed assignment of teachers to the business academy and prevented academy teachers from having a common period during the day for planning their program. Similar problems impeded the start-up of a computer academy at Castlemont High School, which also opened in 1986. In spite of the difficulties, the business and computer academies are both becoming realities. McClymonds High School is also the site of a law and government academy that opened in 1991. In addition, a performing arts academy began operating at Skyline High School in 1989, and a visual arts academy started at Oakland High School in 1991. As of 1991, therefore, a total of eight academies were offering choices to students in all of Oakland's six high schools.

High-Quality Work Experience

One of the key elements of the academy model is paid jobs related to students' coursework. This is intended to help students see the connection between what they do in school and what happens in the world of respectable careers. The importance of related work experience may be greatest for inner-city students because they are more likely to lack adult role models who obtained good jobs as a result of their schooling. Convincing them of the value of school therefore may depend more on their own experience in a good job.

Oakland career academies have been able to provide high-quality work experience for their students. In the summer of 1991 questionnaires were given to students in the four academies receiving support from the Oakland Redevelopment Authority (Rubin, Gibson, and Stern, 1992). Thirty-two questionnaires were completed by students from the health academy, twenty-nine from the media academy, seven from the business academy, and four from the pre-engineering academy. Table 7.1 shows some of the responses. For purposes of comparison, Table 7.1 also shows responses from high school students in other parts of the country in the fall of both 1988 and 1989 (Stone, Stern, Hopkins, and McMillion, 1990). The comparison study included students who were employed in school-supervised work experience (SSWE) programs (mainly cooperative vocational education) and students at the same schools who were employed in non-school-supervised jobs (NSWE).

Table 7.1 shows Oakland Academy students reporting a stronger perception than other students that their jobs are related to what they do in school. The only exception is in the use of math on the job. Among the students from other parts of the country, SSWE participants report a stronger relationship between school and work than do their schoolmates who were employed in NSWE. On five of the seven questions

Table 7.1. Relatedness of Work Experience to School.[a]

	Oakland (n=72)	SSWE (n=362)	NSWE (n=600)
"My job gives me a chance to practice what I learned in school." (percent "very true")	38	24	6
"What I have learned in school helps me do better on my job." (percent "strongly agree")	39	12	3
"My job provides information about things I am studying in school." (percent "strongly agree")	28	10	3
"School makes me realize how important it is to learn to do things well on my job." (percentage "strongly agree")	49	13	7
"My job has made me realize how important it is to learn and do well in school." (percent "strongly agree")	48	23[b]	16[b]
"Do you use reading on this job?" (percent "yes")	86	59	36
"Do you use math on this job?" (percent "yes")	45	70	58
"Do you use writing on this job?" (percent "yes")	86	73	48

[a] As reported by Oakland Academy and other high school students in school-supervised (SSWE) and non-school-supervised (NSWE) jobs.

[b] Question read, "My job has taught me the importance of getting a good education."

for which Oakland Academy students' percentages are highest, the difference between the Oakland students and SSWE students elsewhere exceeds the difference between SSWE and NSWE students. Compared to other working students, they report that they make more use on the job of what they have learned in school, except math. More of the academy students also report that their job informs and motivates their work in school.

These differences occur in spite of the fact that other questions, which asked about involvement of teachers or other school staff members in visiting the job, writing a training plan, and evaluating students' performance on the job, indicated less direct school supervision of students' work experience in the Oakland Academies than in the SSWE programs elsewhere. Apparently Oakland Academy students see a strong connection between school and their summer work experience even though their summer jobs are not closely monitored by school staff.

The focused academy curriculum, complemented by direct contacts with employers in the field before students actually apply for a paid job, evidently prepares Oakland Academy students to see their summer jobs as a direct extension and application of what they do in high school. For these students there is no longer such a sharp boundary between school and the world outside.

The East Side Electronics Academies, San Jose

The East Side Union High School District in San Jose is located at the southern end of the Silicon Valley, about twenty-five miles south of the Sequoia district and fifty miles from San Francisco. It is one of the veteran academy sites in California, having established two academies in the fall of 1985 with the first round of state-supported replications. A third academy grant was awarded to the district at the start of the 1990–91 school year. All three programs focus on electronics.

The electronics academies in the East Side San Jose District have proven to be among the most successful in the state, for a variety of reasons. They have enjoyed particularly strong district support, from both the superintendent and the director of career services, who is a leader in vocational education in the state and a member of the State Council on Vocational Education. They have also enjoyed strong business support through a coalition of Silicon Valley companies that includes Hewlett-Packard, IBM, Lockheed, and Xerox. The ways in which these academies have developed and employed this private sector support is of particular interest. Related to this is the unusual degree of interest these academies have shown in serious evaluation, which they view as critical for maintaining such business support.

San Jose is the largest city in the Bay Area. With its roughly 750,000 residents it now surpasses its more famous neighbor to the north, San Francisco. The East Side district is a large one with a broad spectrum of students. Ethnically, its students are approximately 49 percent Hispanic, 25 percent white, 20 percent Asian/Pacific Islander, and 6 percent African American.

Electronics is the hardware side of computers and other electronic equipment, as opposed to computer use and applications, which make up the software side. Students in the electronics academies learn about how electronic machines work, are assembled, and can be repaired. They study electricity, magnetism, conductors and insulators, resistance and resistors, components, switches, and circuits. Activities include learning about and using basic electronic equipment and terminology, repairing small appliances, assembling circuit boards, and assembling and testing various electronic devices. There had been a focus on electronics in the district for some years, one so strong that the state curriculum guidelines in the field were developed by teachers from this district.

Recruiting Mentors

When the first two East Side electronics academies began in 1985, the district decided to experiment with a variation on the three-year school-within-a-school structure. Rather than admit students each year at the sophomore level, it chose to select a full complement of over a hundred students at the freshman level and provide a four-year program for them. District officials reasoned that this would help reduce its high dropout rate in the ninth grade and retain students beyond the difficult transition from middle to high schools. The district also felt that if the program could be successful over three years, it could be even more successful over four.

This experiment caused problems. It worked reasonably well the first year, and in fact it brought to bear a full complement of academy teachers from the start. However, when it came time to recruit mentors during the sophomore year, instead of the usual number required for one class level (around forty), the program was faced with recruiting over one hundred for each school—more than two hundred in all. This proved to be a monumental task.

To meet the challenge the district hired a full-time assistant to the career services director, whose sole job was to develop private sector support for the academies. A graduate student interested in alternative programs for at-risk youth, she dedicated herself to making the academies successful. Armed with boundless energy and a positive outlook, she approached the job in a variety of ways. She made use of any business contacts the programs' teachers and administrators had. She visited the Peninsula Academies to the north and borrowed some of their contacts while learning about their techniques for building employer support.

She also approached companies on her own, working through human resource or community relations departments to make her case for the program. After several months she found more than the needed number of mentors, many of whom became advocates for the academies in their companies, which led to other kinds of support as well. (In part to avoid the necessity of recruiting so many mentors all at once, the district has since reverted to the usual three-year academy structure.)

Continuing Business Support

Business support for the East Side academies has continued since that time and can be seen in many ways. There is a strong steering committee, which serves all three academies. The academies have an active program of speakers and field trips each year. The mentor program continues to thrive. During the 1990–91 school year 137 mentors participated, enough for all the academy juniors, most of the seniors, and a few sophomores. While the recession harmed the work experience program that year, thirty-nine students were placed in summer jobs.

The district estimates that nearly five hundred days of time were volunteered by business representatives during the

1990–91 school year, the bulk of them spread about equally across four roles: serving as mentors, arranging job placements for students, supervising students on the job, and organizing and leading field trips. Using a formula based on the salaries of the corporate people involved in these activities, the district estimates the value of this time to be over $200,000.

Perhaps most impressive, for the past four years the supporting companies have provided a full-time "loaned business liaison" to coordinate employer involvement for the East Side academies. A Hewlett-Packard employee, this woman began her efforts during the 1987–88 school year with a two-year commitment. Supporting businesses have renewed this commitment twice, and she has continued ever since. Her position is co-funded by several companies. She is based at the district offices and works closely with the career services director. She coordinates field trips and speakers, the mentor program, and the work experience program. In recent years she has also come into demand as a speaker and workshop leader for other academies.

Importance of Evaluation

The original two East Side academies, at Independence and Silver Creek High Schools, were evaluated from 1985 through 1988 as part of the statewide assessment that included the Oakland health academy. Both academies demonstrated a strong pattern of program effects for their participants in this evaluation. By the third year, Silver Creek High School academy students outperformed their comparison group counterparts on all measures examined, and three-fourths of these differences reached statistical significance. Independence High School academy students outperformed their comparison group counterparts on three-fourths of the measures examined, and a third of these differences reached statistical significance (the previous year all differences had favored the program students at a statistically significant level).

While some districts and high schools react defensively

to proposed evaluation, the East Side academies were enthusiastic. They subsequently found the results useful in developing the employer support the programs needed to operate. In fact, the district disseminated the statewide evaluations to its many business supporters to demonstrate the effect the program was having on students. Business representatives reacted with surprise and delight. While they were used to evaluating their own efforts and products for a competitive marketplace, they did not expect it to come from the schools.

As a result, the East Side academies have continued to conduct their own academy evaluations since the statewide one ended in 1988. These yearly reports contain information on student performance, comparing the academy students with their school and district counterparts on retention and graduation rates, attendance, and credits. The results continue to show strongly positive program effects. The reports also contain descriptive information on enrollments, displayed by gender and ethnicity, and on program income and spending, summer jobs, mentorships, and other activities. Finally, the reports show progress toward that year's program goals and present a new set of goals for the coming year.

East Side district officials also argue each year for the reinstitution of a statewide evaluation system for all partnership academies. Partly as a result, statewide data were collected following the 1990–91 school year on academy students' retention, attendance, credits, and grades. While no comparison figures were collected, this system will henceforward provide yearly information that shows how academy students are performing in California. East Side is also lending its support to the idea of conducting a true random-assignment evaluation of academies.

As discussed elsewhere in this book, academies are dependent on a solid school-business partnership if they are to succeed. The East Side electronics academies, which enjoy an ideal location to develop such a partnership, have taken this mission seriously and capitalized on this opportunity. As a result, they have seen their academy students flourish, aided by the many speakers they hear, their frequent field trips to companies, their mentors, and their work experience positions. Recognizing that the best way to maintain this strong business support is to demonstrate the programs' positive effects on students, district officials have used their own resources to continue evaluating their academies. In the process, they have shown how helpful good evaluation can be in maintaining the school-business partnership on which academies must be founded.

Pasadena

A recent addition to the family of partnership academies in California is the series of programs in Pasadena, north of Los Angeles. Pasadena Unified High School District has used the academy model as a foundation to launch a broad high school restructuring effort throughout the district. It has established a whole series of academies in different fields, secured broad and deep private sector and community support, linked academic and vocational curricula, and seriously approached related staff development needs. Of particular interest are Pasadena's student selection criteria and procedures, links between academies and postsecondary institutions, and efforts to develop a set of standards and assessments around each program.

Historically, Pasadena was an upper-middle-class white community, but over the past twenty years this has changed. During the 1970s there was a significant inflow of African American residents, and large numbers of Hispanics and Armenians arrived in the 1980s. All these groups have been in lower economic ranges, giving the district a predominantly lower-middle-class distribution, with a somewhat bipolar distribution given the remaining whites. Today the district student population is approximately 36 percent Hispanic, 34 percent African American, 19 percent white, 3 percent Asian, and 8 percent other.

Pasadena Unified School District has established six career academies in its four high schools over the past two years and plans to begin four more during the 1992–93 school year. Only two are supported by state partnership academy grants. The ten academies are in the fields of health, high technology, finance, space, computers, graphic arts, environmental studies, public service, teaching, and design. Since each academy operates as a magnet program for the whole district, the ten academies give Pasadena students a wide variety of career themes from which to choose.

Student Recruitment and Preparation

As discussed earlier, partnership academies in California generally target an at-risk population of students, those performing below their potential and thought likely to drop out before graduating. Pasadena has expanded this criterion to include a broader cross section of students, based primarily on interest in the field of training. As an instrument for high school restructuring, this is one direction in which academies can move to have broader impact.

The Pasadena district has also established a set of entry requirements in basic academic fields for its academies, and it has made these known to students in earlier grades who may be interested in entering an academy in grade 10. The purpose is to extend the motivational benefit of the academies to these earlier grades and retain students in school until they can enter an academy. For this purpose Pasadena has developed a set of "Pre-Academy Portfolio Requirements" that define what students must do to be eligible for the program.

To assist students who are interested but are not ready to enter an academy, Pasadena has also developed a series of pre-academy courses. One of these is a six-week summer course, part of a "Comprehensive Math and Science Program" (CMSP) developed by Columbia University, offered by California State University, Los Angeles. Using a "ground zero" approach that assumes virtually no knowledge of math, this program has had great success in bringing ninth-grade students up to a pre-algebra level, ready for their respective academies. Over one hundred students participated in the summer of 1991, and more than 80 percent earned grades of A

or B. Other courses underway or planned for pre-academy
students include a computer skills course taught at Pasadena
City college and a language development course for limited-
English-proficient students.

Postsecondary Linkages

A common recommendation for high school restructuring is
"tech prep," a focused course of study that combines (at least)
the last two years of high school and a two-year program at a
community college. Such sequences permit students to
achieve a higher level of technical education in less time.

The Pasadena district has developed an extensive
arrangement with its nearest community college, Pasadena
City College (PCC), to provide accelerated programs for students in several academies. The district has also developed
links with several four-year colleges that will allow students
to transfer easily to baccalaureate programs in academy fields.
Participating colleges include California State University, Los
Angeles, Occidental College, and the California State of
Technology.

For example, students in the computer academy will be
required, during their junior and senior years, to take one-
year "practical" courses through the Los Angeles County
Regional Occupational Program or PCC. Juniors and seniors
in the finance academy will take advanced finance or business
courses each semester at PCC. Their counterparts in the space
academy will take a laser technology course each of those
years provided by PCC but delivered on their high school
campus.

The graphic arts academy at Pasadena High School
illustrates how a "tech prep" articulated program will work,
in this case with ties to Pasadena City College and Cal State
Los Angeles. The grade 10 courses are taught at Pasadena
High School. In grade 11 students take a one-year advanced
course in graphic arts at PCC, and during grade 12 they continue with other advanced graphic arts courses there. Upon
graduation they can enter the PCC program with up to

twenty-four units of advanced credit, allowing them to complete the community college graphic arts degree in one year and making them eligible for a technical position in the field. They can then choose to go on to Cal State Los Angeles for a baccalaureate degree, leading to a management position in the field.

Certifying Students' Achievement

Another frequent recommendation for improving students' post-high school transition is establishment of standards that are recognized by employers. Such standards would allow schools to plan their curriculum and students to plan their course selection in a more logical and coherent way. For instance the *America's Choice* report (National Center on Education and the Economy, 1990) calls for a midcourse high school assessment that would determine whether students have gained the necessary core academic skills to allow them to branch out into more career-defined directions; it suggests linking such an assessment to a "Certificate of Initial Mastery."

For its academies Pasadena is developing an end-of-eleventh-grade assessment. Students who pass will receive a Certificate of Initial Mastery. The reason for delaying the test until the end of eleventh grade is that it will allow the academies two years to develop students' skills. Also the summer following eleventh grade is the first time academy students will have work experience positions; the assessment results and certificate will be used when students apply for these positions.

Pasadena's Certificate of Initial Mastery will define benchmarks of several types:

- Strict attendance ("industry, not school, standards")
- Work ethics and habits
- Exploratory work experience requirements
- Oral communication
- Written communication
- Algebra and its applications
- Other basic academic skills

Students will be allowed to progress through these assessments in both their sophomore and junior years by building portfolios. Only those who meet all the standards will be allowed to apply for summer internships after their junior year, and every effort will be made to ensure that these students receive such internships.

Pasadena is also developing a specialized high school transcript and diploma that will show employers the demonstrated skills and accomplishments of students who have graduated from an academy. This will be adapted to each of the various academies, so that, for example, the transcripts of graduates from the health academy will display all of their health-related courses, their internships, and their skills as they relate to various health field jobs. District officials are working on this effort in cooperation with the Educational Testing Service's Worklink project, for which Pasadena is one of a few pilot sites. Worklink is being designed to provide employers with useful information on students' high school performance based on a combination of transcript information, tailored testing, and references from teachers and employers.

ALIVE: Academies and Beyond

Because of all these efforts the Pasadena district has become something of a leader in California in its efforts to build programs around the academy model and improve its transition-to-work system. It has received a number of both state and private grants to help with these efforts, and during the 1991–92 school year it plans to bring together information on its programs into a replication guide for use in other districts. The series of academies and related efforts has been given the name Academic Learning Integrating Vocational Education (ALIVE). The model is based on the following features:

- *Defined entry-level skills* in grades 7 through 9, in effect entrance requirements for an academy, to be measured through a portfolio system. This allows the academies to reach down to lower grade levels with incentives and direction.

- *Pre-academy courses* for students interested in entering academies who lack sufficient skills, offered during the summer following ninth grade. These are taught in prestigious settings—namely, Pasadena City College and California Institute of Technology—and draw on the facilities and staffs of those institutions.

- *A series of academies focusing on various career fields* (high technology, health, computers, finance, graphic arts, environmental studies, education, public service, and design) that are healthy and tied to local industries. These are located in the district's various high schools, so that each such school has at least one academy already and will have several over time.

- *Substantial private sector support* in planning and supporting the various academies. This includes not only a role in defining the technical skills to be taught but also financial assistance. All the usual academy forms of involvement are included: speakers, field trips, mentors, and work experience positions. In some cases, the work experience has been expanded into something approaching a true apprenticeship experience.

- *Close relationships with the Los Angeles County Regional Occupational Program and Pasadena Community College,* allowing easy transfer of academy students to further training through what are in effect 2 + 2 arrangements.

- *Close cooperation with area colleges,* including Occidental College, California Technical Institute, California State University, Los Angeles, and Pasadena City College, in planning the curriculum and outcome skills of participants as well as providing structured 3 + 2 + 2 arrangements for academy graduates to move through community college into baccalaureate programs.

- *A specialized high school diploma and a related transcript* that spells out the skills needed to succeed in each academy field, and pilot testing of the Educational Testing Service's Worklink system to help in the assessment of these skills and in providing useful employment information to businesses.

Parts of a Coherent Effort

Descriptions of these four districts suggest how academy programs develop unique personalities as a result of the particular opportunities and resources that are present in their local environments. These district portraits also illustrate key features of the academy model: integrated curriculum, related work experience, mentors, and enlargement of students' options for work or further education after high school. In all four of these districts, as in all successful academies, these and other features of the model achieve coherence in a community of students, teachers, employers, and parents who use these programmatic ideas to advance students' motivation, knowledge, and career success.

Part Three:

The Future

EIGHT

⚔ ○ ⚔

Academies
and the Reconstruction
of American High Schools

Career academies point the way toward resolving chronic dilemmas of American high schools. The Philadelphia and California academies have focused on helping potential dropouts finish high school by offering a high-powered form of vocational education integrated with an academic core. They have shown on a small scale, with some of the most resistant students, what might be accomplished for all students by redesigning the high school in its entirety. The useful implications of the career academy model extend far beyond vocational education and at-risk students. Other academies now proliferating under the leadership of the National Academy Foundation are extending the model to all kinds of students, including many who are clearly college-bound. The Philadelphia and California academies themselves are evolving in this direction.

Students who choose an academy commit themselves to a demanding program that prepares them for work or further education. While serving some students who are at risk of dropping out, academies also maintain students' option of going to college and thereby avoid being stigmatized as second-rate programs. The career-oriented curriculum, extensive contacts with employers, and opportunities for part-time and summer jobs related to their coursework stimulate students' interest. Keeping a relatively small group of students and teachers together for several years provides social support and a sense of identity. These and other features of the academy model, if applied to the high school as a whole, could help that troubled institution solve some of its fundamental, long-standing problems.

Keeping It Together: Threats to Academies

If they are to play a part in reshaping the American high school, academies must show they have staying power. Once initiated, academy programs often face continuing threats to their survival and integrity. Some of these problems were discussed in Chapter Five.

Sheer entropy is one major threat. As a school-within-a-school, the academy stands out from its surroundings. Block rostering academy students requires special attention from administrators who make up the master schedule and cooperation from counselors who assign individual students to courses. Ensuring that academy teachers have a preparation period scheduled at the same time also calls for special dispensation. Even when administrators want to support the academy program, these scheduling problems are not trivial.

High rates of mobility among both teachers and students in many high schools also make it difficult to maintain academy programs. Administrative policies usually aim to prevent classes from becoming too small, but this can be difficult if several students leave the academy program during the school year and other students are not readily available to replace them. Similarly, if academy teachers leave there may not be other teachers available who possess the necessary combination of talents and interest. Administrators have to keep shoring up the program against these forces of erosion.

Another kind of threat is the temptation to stratify programs according to students' perceived level of academic ability, creating some academies for students considered smart and others for those deemed not as smart. Tracking has become so prevalent in high schools that many teachers have never learned to manage classrooms with both fast and slow students. Segregating students by perceived academic ability or expected educational attainment—"college-bound" versus "non-college-bound"—has become the path of least resistance. But programs for students who are assumed to be second-rate tend to suffer from diminished expectations, low morale, and underachievement. The effectiveness of academies in motivating students, and their value as exemplars of high school reform, depend on treating all students as potential high achievers, keeping open everyone's options for further education, and resisting the temptation to segregate by perceived ability.

Lack of money is another ever-present danger—the chronic poverty of school budgets, especially in central city neighborhoods and low-income rural communities. Where there are not enough resources to hire qualified teachers or maintain school buildings, it is difficult to provide the extras that make an academy program possible: extra preparation time, staff development, special equipment, administrative time to recruit mentors and arrange job placements for students, and the other large and small items that add up to hundreds of dollars per pupil. Existing academies have depended on outside grants: in California from the state legislature, in Philadelphia from local businesses, and elsewhere from the National Academy Foundation. Long-term viability of academies will depend on finding long-term financial support.

Sources of Support in the 1990 Perkins Act

One major source of funds for academies is the federal program for vocational education, currently authorized by the amendments in the Carl D. Perkins Act (U.S. Congress, 1990). At least $1 billion a year are authorized under Title II for the basic grant to states. Section 235 stipulates, in part, that these

"funds shall be used to provide vocational education in programs that . . . integrate academic and vocational education . . . through coherent sequences of courses." This
program is tailor-made for career academies.

Integrating Academic and Vocational Education

The mandate to combine vocational and academic education
represents a ninety-degree turn from the historical direction
of federally funded vocational education. Whether to organize
vocational education as a separate track or teach it together
with academic subjects was the subject of intense controversy
before 1917, when the Smith-Hughes Act first provided federal
aid for vocational education (Lazerson and Grubb, 1974). But
the Smith-Hughes Act (U.S. Congress, 1917) came down on
the side of segregation by defining vocational education as
preparation for occupations not ordinarily requiring a bachelor's or advanced degree. This split vocational education from
preparation for college. In the decades that followed, the continued flow of federal funds reinforced rigid separation
between the college and vocational tracks, each with its own
courses, teachers, administrators, regulations, bureaucrats, lob-
byists, and legislative advocates. From time to time, critics
revived the controversy, arguing that tracking was undemo-
cratic and that vocational training was too narrow. But until
the 1980s there was never any widespread movement to reinte-
grate academic and vocational education.

The extent of current efforts to reunite vocational and
academic instruction has been described by Grubb and others
(1991, pp. 11–12): "Several states have undertaken statewide
efforts to integrate vocational and academic education, among
them Ohio, Oregon, and New York; others have invested in
pilot projects, including California, Washington, Idaho, and
Florida. A consortium of more than thirty schools in the
Southeast, part of the SREB [Southeast Regional Education
Board], has pledged its allegiance to principles designed to
upgrade the vocational curriculum and improve the basic
education of vocational students (Bottoms and Presson, 1989).

The approach of 'academies'—schools-within-schools—has been tried throughout the country from its inception in Philadelphia to its extensive replication in California. Numerous school districts have initiated their own changes, generating new curricula and new ways of organizing the high school; and magnet high schools oriented around vocational areas and single-occupation high schools have provided yet other ways in which academic education might comfortably and naturally be infused into vocational programs. Curriculum development has proceeded as well: A number of publishers now offer materials to incorporate basic skills into vocational courses, and 'applied academics' curricula—versions of academic courses such as physics, math, and English with more occupationally relevant content—have proliferated."

In this context, academies are one of several models for integrating academic and vocational education. Grubb and his associates (pp. 15–17) have identified eight distinct methods in current use, ranging from relatively simple to more complex:

- Vocational teachers incorporating more academic content in their courses
- Academic and vocational teachers teaming up to enhance academic content in vocational programs
- Making academic courses more vocationally relevant
- Curricular alignment, either coordinating academic and vocational courses to teach related content at the same time or arranging courses in a logical sequence over time
- Senior projects involving work-related applications of academic subjects
- The academy model, using a school-within-a-school format to give some students an integrated curriculum with links to employers
- Occupational high schools and magnet schools, entire high schools delivering an integrated curriculum for a set of related occupations
- Occupational clusters, "career paths," and majors within comprehensive high schools, offering all students a choice

among several course sequences, each sequence combining academic and vocational courses around a particular occupational focus

As this typology suggests, the academy model can be generalized by applying it to a whole high school in at least two different ways: either organizing the whole school around a single set of related occupations, or creating parallel course sequences reflecting different occupational specializations. In other words, either make the whole high school one big academy, or organize it as a set of smaller academies where each student chooses one. As examples of the one-big-academy model, Grubb and others describe a health professions high school and an agriculture high school. They refer to additional examples described by Mitchell, Russell, and Benson (1989): New York's Aviation High School, the High School of Fashion Industries, and Murray Bergtraum High School for Business Careers, as well as Chicago's High School for Agricultural Sciences. Although single-theme vocational high schools are much larger than academies organized as schools-within-schools, the social and emotional advantages of small size could be regained by dividing a one-big-academy high school into separate "houses." In this context, the career theme would be the same for all houses.

Grubb and others (1991) also provide case studies of three comprehensive high schools that have organized themselves, in effect, as groups of academies with different themes. One example of a high school that is similar to a collection of academies is in Woodland, California. In ninth grade each student chooses one of six "career paths": agriculture and natural resources; arts and communications; business and marketing; health, home, and recreation; industrial technology and engineering; or social, human, and governmental services. Counselors help the student plan a coherent sequence of courses so that, as in an academy, much of the coursework is related to the occupational theme. Each career path leads either to employment immediately following high school or to further education. Interestingly, after organizing the curriculum around occupational themes, Woodland has found that more of its graduating students are now attending college. One difference between Woodland and the academy model, however, is that students in Woodland's career paths are not scheduled as classroom cohorts who take several classes together.

Generalizing the curricular principles of academies to the whole high school is one way to establish them on a more permanent footing. Organizing the whole school as one big academy eliminates the difficulties that arise from the block rostering of students, simultaneous preparation periods for teachers, and the other problems of maintaining a small-scale school-within-a-school. On the other hand, the benefits for students of belonging to a smaller unit may be worth the effort. If the whole high school is organized as a collection of academies, with the same or different career themes, the problems of maintaining small scale remain but they apply to everyone, not just to a special few, and they become part of the school's routine. Either way, the forces of erosion and entropy that threaten academies as schools-within-schools become less dangerous.

Whether they remain schools-within-schools or are generalized to whole high schools, academy programs are exactly the kind of program Title II of the 1990 Perkins amendments was intended to promote. This law therefore should give a big boost to the establishment and maintenance of academies.

Tech Prep

Title III of the 1990 Perkins amendments provides money for various special programs. One of these, "Tech prep," also has a strong affinity with academies. The 1990 act authorizes special grants for secondary schools to join with two-year colleges or apprenticeship programs for the purpose of creating new tech prep curricula. These encompass the last two years of high school and two years of postsecondary education in what is often called a 2 + 2 sequence, "with a common core of required proficiency in mathematics, science, communications, and technologies designed to lead to an associate degree or certificate in a specific career field" (U.S. Congress, 1990, section 344).

Like academies, tech prep programs are intended to combine academic and vocational courses that have traditionally been kept apart in separate tracks. Dale Parnell, an early and influential proponent of the tech prep concept, wants it to "break down the walls between vocational education and academic education" (1990). The Illinois State Board of Education (1990, p. 1) has adopted the following definition: "Illinois Tech-prep represents an educational track that integrates college preparatory coursework with a rigorous technical education concentration. It is a planned sequence of courses, both academic and technical, that begins at ninth grade and is articulated with a post-secondary experience leading to an associate degree. Because Tech-prep prepares students for a lifetime of learning, it also provides preparation for advanced education such as a four-year baccalaureate degree. Tech-prep prepares students with the skills and competencies necessary to meet employers' performance standards not only for entry level jobs, but also for career advancement."

The importance of integrated curriculum is also asserted by a tech prep program called PACE (Partnership for Academic and Career Education) in Pendleton, South Carolina, which lists as one of its goals to "increase students' motivation to learn academic concepts by using career-related examples from business, industrial/engineering technology, health, and public service fields in the teaching of math, English, and science courses" (American Association of Community and Junior Colleges, 1989). As indicated in these statements, the rationale for tech prep is similar to the theory behind vocational academies: an integrated curriculum presents academic course material in a way that is more meaningful to students, in order to prepare them for both employment and further education.

The Illinois definition explicitly calls for tech prep to begin in grade 9, thus including all four years of high school instead of only the last two as specified in federal law. This is an example of a 4 + 2 program, which seems to be a common variation on the 2 + 2 theme. Similarly, the PACE program operated by Tri-County Technical College and neighboring high schools in Pendleton, South Carolina, provides "a coordinated, sequenced series of academic and vocational courses starting in grade 9 and continuing through completion of two-year college occupational certificate, diploma or associate degree programs" (American Association of Community and Junior College, 1989). Another example of 4 + 2 is the tech prep program offered by Richmond Community College and surrounding high schools in Richmond, North Carolina. School officials there explain that if they waited until junior year to recruit for tech prep they would not find enough students who had completed prerequisite courses, particularly algebra (Dornsife, 1990). This appears to be a common view.

Another variation is 2 + 2 + 2, which combines the last two years of high school with two years of community college and then two more years at a four-year college, culminating in a bachelor's degree. An example is the ACE (Achieving College Education) option offered at South Mountain Community College, part of the Maricopa Community College system in Phoenix, Arizona. "The goal of the program is to increase the number of students who achieve bachelor's degrees after successfully completing high school and community college" (South Mountain Community College, 1989). The program permits high school students to take college classes offered at local high schools. It facilitates the eventual transfer to four-year college by directing students into community college courses that have already been pre-approved for lower-division credit at the state university. ACE specifically targets minority and economically disadvantaged students and offers additional support services including financial aid information and parent involvement.

Once a community college has designed a tech prep program with local high schools in a particular technical specialty, it becomes easier to design programs in other specialties. Community colleges are thus offering diverse tech prep options, generalizing the model across the curriculum. Richmond Community College and Richmond County, North Carolina, pioneered with 4 + 2 programs in engineering, health/human services, and business. Similarly, Sandhills Community College and Moore County, North Carolina, offer 4 + 2 sequences in business and marketing, engineering and industry, and health and human services. Bristol Community College and two local high schools in New Bedford, Massachusetts, have developed tech prep programs in engineering technologies and business technologies. In Anchorage, Alaska, the Anchorage School District and the University of Alaska, Anchorage, are offering 4 + 2 versions of tech prep in aviation maintenance, electronics, welding, architectural and engineering technology, food service, and home economics/ fashion merchandising.

According to the National Tech-Prep Clearinghouse, as of June 1990 there were 122 tech prep programs operating in thirty-three states. Three states had legislated mandates of their own, and six others were considering them. Some of these existing programs may represent an older form of articulation rather than the new definition of tech prep in federal law.

As envisioned in federal law, tech prep denotes a coherent four-year curriculum leading to an associate degree in a technical field of work. Within the high school, tech prep is meant to be more rigorous, high-powered, and prestigious than the "unfocused and watered-down general education curriculum" into which many middle-quartile high school students have drifted, argues Parnell (1990). In Richmond County, North Carolina, where the tech prep option was introduced in 1985–86, approximately 30 percent of high school students (grades 9 through 12) were opting for it in 1990–91, while enrollment in the pre-college track was also approximately 30 percent—up from 25 percent in 1985–86 and 1986–87 (Dornsife, 1990). The name "tech prep" stands alongside "college prep" as a high-status option, designed to "raise the self-esteem level of general and vocational track students by enabling them to identify with a program that has direction, status, and visible support from local employers," in the words of the PACE program (American Association of Community and Junior Colleges, 1989).

Fueled by the 1990 Perkins amendments (the appropriation for tech prep was $63.4 million in fiscal 1991), this idea is likely to spread. It would be logical for an academy program to constitute the high school part of the sequence. In fact, some academies have already negotiated with their local community colleges to become formally linked in tech prep arrangements. This kind of linkage helps secure a long-term role for the academies (Stern, 1991).

Academies Fit with Other Reforms

The Perkins Act directly pertains to vocational education, which is only part of the curriculum in high schools and two-year colleges—and it controls only the federal share, which is a small fraction of the total expenditure on vocational education. Although changes in the 1990 Perkins Act have great historic significance, the act is only the tip of a long tail trying to wag the large dog of high school reform. Yet other powerful forces are also working for reform. Some of these are pulling in the same direction as the new Perkins Act and the academy movement.

Greater Collaboration Between Schools and Employers

America 2000 is the Bush administration's national strategy for education (U.S. Department of Education, 1991). It is designed to solve some of the same central problems addressed by the academies: "[E]ight years after the National Commission on Excellence in Education declared us a 'Nation at Risk,' we haven't turned things around in education. Almost all our education trend lines are flat. . . . Meanwhile, our employers cannot hire enough qualified workers. Immense sums are spent on remedial training, much of it at the college level. Companies export skilled work—or abandon projects that require it" (pp. 5-6).

To solve the problems of education, America 2000 proposes to rely increasingly on employers themselves. For example, the New American Schools Development Corporation is a private, nonprofit corporation chartered to collect private contributions for "a new generation of American schools," America 2000's main programmatic initiative.

Involvement of business in America 2000 continues a trend that grew during the 1980s. While employers traditionally have acted as advisers to local vocational education programs, the 1980s witnessed a growing number of businesses and business organizations forming partnerships with local schools. Growth of academies was one example of new business initiatives. Generally, employers' involvement in schools took three forms (Snyder and McMullan, 1987b): efforts targeted directly to students, such as Careers in the Classroom in St. Louis; programs targeted to individual schools, often called "adopt-a-school"; and efforts targeted at entire school districts, such as the Boston Compact. The central motivation for business was to alleviate the perceived shortage of qualified workers. In the words of John Carter, chairman of the National Alliance of Business, "We need workers who are able to think on their feet and learn the job quickly. However, our schools are producing entry-level workers who lack the basic skills necessary to do the jobs that we have available" (National Alliance of Business, 1989, p. 3).

In the 1990s there are some signs of growing recognition that the most productive collaboration between employers and schools requires change not only in the schools but also in workplaces. The most influential statement of this view so far is the *America's Choice* report (National Center on Education and the Economy, 1990), which found that a startling "95 percent of American companies still cling to old forms of work organization. Because most American employers organize work in a way that does not require high skills, they report no shortage of people who have such skills and foresee no such shortage. With some exceptions, the education and skill levels of American workers roughly match the demands of their jobs" (p. 3). There appears to be a vicious cycle: employers continue to use old forms of work organization because they do not expect to be able to hire people with the skills necessary for new, high-performance work systems—while students, who see that few high-performance work organizations now exist, have little incentive to prepare for them.

The 1990s may see the widening of a dialogue that addresses supply and demand together in a coordinated fashion. The essential idea is that improvement must occur jointly in employees' skills and in the organization of work. To compete successfully, producers of goods and services generally must offer higher quality, lower cost, and a quicker response to customers. Proponents contend that this kind of economic performance is best achieved in work organizations that delegate more decision making and problem solving to front-line production workers (Dertouzos, Lester, and Solow, 1989; National Center on Education and the Economy, 1990). Employees in these high-performance work organizations require high levels of skill and knowledge. The present problem is not a short supply of skills for the kinds of jobs that presently exist but scarcity of skills required in the kinds of jobs that will have to be created in much larger numbers if the nation's economy is to regain its competitive edge. Creation of skills and redesign of work go hand in hand.

Academy programs provide a setting in which this new dialogue can take place. Academies have been recognized as outstanding examples of collaboration between employers and schools. The National Alliance of Business awarded the California Peninsula Academies its 1987 Distinguished Performance Award. Public/Private Ventures selected the Philadelphia academies as an exemplary model of business-school partnership (Snyder and McMullan, 1987b). Trust and confidence based on years of successful collaboration will enable academies to play a role in the expanded partnerships between schools and businesses envisioned for the 1990s.

Wider Choice

A prominent feature of America 2000 is its call for "states and localities to adopt comprehensive choice policies" and revision of federal compensatory education (see Chapter One) "to ensure that federal dollars follow the child to whatever extent state and local policies permit" (U.S. Department of Education, 1991, p. 12). These proposals are controversial, and their enactment is uncertain. But choice plans already exist in a number of states, and there is continuing interest in expanding them.

Academies are well-suited as vehicles for choice, whether choice options are narrow or broad. If the political process produces a far-ranging "voucher" plan, where families can use public funds to pay for private schools, the academies provide a model for organizing such schools. If choice remains limited to public schools, the academies have already demonstrated how to organize options within existing public schools. Whatever the legal and administrative structure, the academy model offers a set of viable options.

One serious constraint on choice at the high school level is college entrance requirements. As long as colleges require applicants to have sat for a certain number of semesters in certain classes, schools have only limited leeway to revise curriculum. This issue has not been raised by America 2000 or other reform documents. There are probably two reasons for this omission. First, college and university standards are widely regarded as legitimate. Second, it has not been apparent how to measure attainment of these standards except by time spent sitting in classes.

Without challenging the legitimacy of college and university entrance standards, it is now becoming possible to conceive of other ways to measure their attainment. Currently a great deal of work is going into the design of new methods to assess what students know (Wolf, Bixby, Glenn, and Gardner, 1991). Some of this is based in new findings in cognitive science that authentic knowledge must be measured in a real context. This view is reflected in new methods of assessment proposed by the Secretary's Commission on Achieving Necessary Skills (SCANS) (U.S. Department of Labor, 1991). America 2000 itself is also proposing new American Achievement Tests to monitor students' progress (U.S. Department of Education, 1991, p. 11).

For example, new assessment procedures may create the possibility of deciding whether a high school senior is qualified for college physics by letting her spend several hours in a lab doing physics. It should not matter whether the student learned to do physics by taking a conventional course with a standard textbook or by participating in, say, an automotive academy that included deep study of engines and transmissions. Similarly, students might master high school mathematics in an electronics academy or learn a foreign language by publishing a bilingual newspaper in a media academy. Given new procedures to assess what students know, it is difficult to justify clinging to seat-time as the *only* measure of whether students satisfy course prerequisites for college entrance. Creating the option of using these new procedures instead would give greater leeway to academies and other innovative programs, and would produce a broader range of real curricular choices for high school students.

A Viable Model

Career academies are flourishing because they have succeeded in solving some of the fundamental problems in American high schools: they link school to the world outside, place academic instruction in a practical context, engage students in a learning community, avoid tracking, and prepare students for both work and further education. Benefit-cost analysis has found that the value of one benefit alone—dropout prevention—exceeds the program's incremental cost (Stern, Dayton, Paik, and Weisberg, 1989).

Embodying various curricular themes, academies provide greater choice for diverse students. They have responded to employers' complaints about a lack of qualified workers by involving businesses in partnerships with local schools, and these partnerships provide a context for growing dialogue about simultaneous changes in school and work. The structure of career academies engenders closer collaboration with parents and a more professional role for teachers. The model has been replicated and adapted in various local circumstances. Combining a number of ideas in one coherent program, career academies serve as a tested model for reconstructing American high schools.

Appendix

AMENDED IN ASSEMBLY SEPTEMBER 9, 1987

AMENDED IN ASSEMBLY SEPTEMBER 8, 1987

AMENDED IN ASSEMBLY AUGUST 18, 1987

AMENDED IN SENATE MAY 19, 1987

AMENDED IN SENATE APRIL 8, 1987

SENATE BILL   No. 605

Introduced by Senator Morgan
(Coauthor: Senator McCorquodale)
(Coauthors: Assembly Members Duplissea, O'Connell, Sher,
Speier, and Vasconcellos)

February 25, 1987

An act to amend Sections 54690, 54691, and 54692 of, to
amend the heading of Article 5 (commencing with Section
54690) of Chapter 9 of Part 29 of, to add Sections 54695 and
54696 to, and to repeal and add Sections 54693 and 54694 of,
the Education Code, relating to education, and making an
appropriation therefor.

LEGISLATIVE COUNSEL'S DIGEST

SB 605, as amended, Morgan. Schools: Partnership
Academies.

(1) Existing law makes various findings regarding the
Peninsula Academies Model Program. Existing law requires
the Superintendent of Public Instruction, commencing with
the 1984–85 fiscal year, from funds appropriated for that
purpose, to provide specified apportionments to high school
districts meeting specified eligibility criteria, for purposes of
establishing not more than 10 academies under the Peninsula
Academies Model Program, and to the Sequoia Union High
School District.

This bill would make specific findings regarding the success of the Peninsula Academies Model Program and would provide for the establishment of additional academies, to be known as Partnership Academies. This bill would require the Superintendent of Public Instruction, commencing with the 1987–88 fiscal year, from funds appropriated for that purpose, to issue grants in specified amounts to high school districts meeting specified eligibility criteria for purposes of planning, establishing, and maintaining Partnership Academies. This bill would authorize the superintendent to issue a maximum of 15 grants per year for the 1987–88, 1988–89, 1989–90, and 1990–91 fiscal years. This bill would require the superintendent, when issuing the grants to school districts, to ensure that the grants are equitably distributed among high wealth and low wealth school districts in urban, rural, and suburban areas. This bill would provide for the identification of eligible students, making presentations to prospective students, and selection of students.

(2) Existing law requires the Educational Technology Committee to assist the superintendent and requires the State Department of Education to evaluate the Peninsula Academies Model Program and to report to the Legislature regarding specified issues 2 years after the effective date of the existing law.

This bill would repeal these provisions and instead would require the superintendent to establish eligibility criteria, as specified, for school districts applying for grants, to contract for a 3-year independent review of the effectiveness of Partnership Academies, and to report the results of the review to the Legislature by January 1, 1991. This bill would prohibit a school district from establishing additional academies until the district has successfully operated its existing academy or academies. This bill would also require the superintendent to develop guidelines with respect to the Partnership Academies, as specified.

(3) This bill would appropriate ~~$635,000~~ $535,000 to the State Department of Education for the 1987–88 fiscal year for allocation as specified.

Vote: majority. Appropriation: yes. Fiscal committee: yes. State-mandated local program: no.

The people of the State of California do enact as follows:

1   SECTION 1.   The heading of Article 5 (commencing
2   with Section 54690) of Chapter 9 of Part 29 of the
3   Education Code is amended to read:
4
5   Article 5.   Partnership Academies
6
7   SEC. 2.   Section 54690 of the Education Code is
8   amended to read:
9   54690.   The Legislature hereby finds and declares that
10   the Peninsula Academies Model Program has proven to
11   be an effective school-business partnership program to
12   provide   occupational   training   to   educationally
13   disadvantaged high school students who present a high
14   risk of dropping out of school. "Educationally
15   disadvantaged high school students," for the purposes of
16   this article, means students enrolled in high school who
17   are at-risk of dropping out of school as indicated by at
18   least three of the following four criteria:
19   (a) Past record of irregular attendance.
20   (b) Past record of underachievement (at least one
21   year behind in the coursework for the student's
22   respective grade level).
23   (c) Past record of low motivation or a disinterest in the
24   regular school program.
25   (d) Disadvantaged economically.
26   The Legislature further finds that the success of the
27   program is directly related both to the participation of
28   private   entities   which   have   provided   personnel,
29   equipment, and training positions and to the initial
30   development of the program conducted by the Sequoia
31   Union High School District.
32   The Legislature further finds and declares that
33   although the original Peninsula Academies were
34   established to provide training in the high technology
35   fields of computers and electronics, the model program
36   has been developed successfully in the fields of medicine,
37   finance, and food services, as well as high technology. It
38   is therefore the intent of the Legislature that additional

1 academies, to be known hereafter as Partnership
2 Academies, be established in California.
3   SEC. 3. Section 54691 of the Education Code is
4 amended to read:
5   54691. Commencing with the 1987–88 fiscal year,
6 from the funds appropriated for that purpose, the
7 Superintendent of Public Instruction shall issue grants to
8 school districts maintaining high schools which meet the
9 specifications of Section 54692, for purposes of planning,
10 establishing, and maintaining academies, as follows:
11   (a) For the 1987–88, 1988–89, 1989–90, and 1990–91
12 fiscal years, the superintendent may issue a maximum of
13 15 grants per year, for purposes of planning Partnership
14 Academies and developing the curriculum. The
15 Superintendent of Public Instruction, when issuing the
16 grants to school districts, shall ensure that the grants are
17 equitably distributed among high wealth and low wealth
18 school districts in urban, rural, and suburban areas. Each
19 planning grant shall be in the amount of fifteen thousand
20 dollars ($15,000).
21   (b) For the 1987–88 fiscal year, and each fiscal year
22 thereafter, the superintendent may issue grants for the
23 implementation and maintenance of academies initiated
24 by the Sequoia Union High School District, the Peninsula
25 Academies Model Program, or planned pursuant to
26 subdivision (a). Implementation and maintenance grants
27 shall be calculated in accordance with the following
28 schedule:
29   (1) Districts operating academies established under
30 the Peninsula Academies Model Program or the Sequoia
31 Union High School District may receive seven hundred
32 fifty dollars ($750) per year for each qualified student
33 enrolled in an academy, provided that no more than
34 sixty-seven thousand five hundred dollars ($67,500) may
35 be granted to any one academy for each fiscal year.
36   (2) Districts operating one or more academies may
37 receive two thousand two hundred fifty dollars ($2,250)
38 for each qualified student enrolled in an academy during
39 the first year of that academy's operation, provided that
40 no more than sixty-seven thousand five hundred dollars

1 ($67,500) may be granted to any one academy for the
2 initial year.
3   (3) Districts operating one or more academies may
4 receive one thousand five hundred dollars ($1,500) for
5 each qualified student enrolled in an academy during the
6 second year of that academy's operation, provided that
7 no more than ninety thousand dollars ($90,000) may be
8 granted to any one academy for the second year.
9   (4) Districts operating one or more academies may
10 receive seven hundred fifty dollars ($750) per year for
11 each qualified student enrolled in an academy during the
12 third year and for each year of operation thereafter,
13 provided that no more than sixty-seven thousand five
14 hundred dollars ($67,500) may be granted to any one
15 academy for each fiscal year.
16   (c) For purposes of this article, a qualified student is a
17 student who is enrolled in an academy for the 10th, 11th,
18 or 12th grade, successfully completes a school year in the
19 academy with an attendance record of no less than 80
20 percent positive attendance, and obtains 90 percent of
21 the credits each academic year in courses that are
22 required for graduation.
23   (d) At the end of each school year, school districts that
24 have been approved to operate academies pursuant to
25 this article shall certify the following information to the
26 Superintendent of Public Instruction:
27   (1) The number of qualified students enrolled during
28 the just completed school year, by grade level, for each
29 academy operated by the district.
30   (2) The operation of each academy in accordance with
31 this article, including Sections 54692 and 54694.
32   (3) The amount of matching funds and the dollar
33 value of in-kind support made available to each academy
34 in accordance with subdivisions (a) and (b) of Section
35 54692.
36   (e) The superintendent shall adjust each school
37 district's grant in accordance with the certification made
38 to him or her pursuant to subdivision (d) or in
39 accordance with any discrepancies to the certification
40 that may be revealed by audit. Notwithstanding the

1   provisions of this section, the superintendent may
2   advance the funding as he or she deems appropriate to
3   districts that are approved to operate, or plan to operate
4   Partnership Academies.
5   (f) Funds granted to school districts pursuant to this
6   article may be expended without regard to fiscal year.
7   SEC. 4. Section 54692 of the Education Code is
8   amended to read:
9   54692. In order to be eligible to receive funding
10 pursuant to this article, a district shall provide all of the
11 following:
12   (a) An amount equal to a 100 percent match of all
13 funds received pursuant to this article, in the form of
14 direct and in-kind support provided by the district.
15   (b) An amount equal to a 100 percent match of all
16 funds received pursuant to this article, in the form of
17 direct and in-kind support provided by participating
18 companies or other private sector organizations.
19   (c) An assurance that each Partnership Academy will
20 be established as a "school within a school" in the same
21 manner as the Peninsula Academies Model Programs.
22   (d) Assurance that each academy student will be
23 provided with:
24   (1) Instruction in at least three academic subjects each
25 regular school term that prepares the student for a
26 regular high school diploma. When possible, these
27 subjects should relate to the occupational field of the
28 academy.
29   (2) A "laboratory class" related to the academy's
30 occupational field.
31   (3) A class schedule which limits the attendance to the
32 classes required in paragraphs (1) and (2) to pupils of the
33 academy.
34   (4) A mentor from the business community during the
35 pupil's 11th grade year.
36   (5) A job related to the academy's occupational field
37 or work experience to improve employment skills, during
38 the summer following the 11th grade. A student that
39 must attend summer school for purposes of completing
40 graduation requirements is exempt from this paragraph.

1   (6) Additional motivational activities with private
2 sector involvement to encourage academic and
3 occupational preparation.
4   SEC. 5.   Section 54693 of the Education Code is
5 repealed.
6   SEC. 6.   Section 54693 is added to the Education Code,
7 to read:
8   54693.   The Superintendent of Public Instruction shall
9 establish eligibility criteria for school districts that apply
10 for grants pursuant to this article. When establishing
11 criteria, the superintendent shall consider the
12 commitment and need of the applicant district. The
13 superintendent may consider district indicators of need
14 such as the number or percent of pupils in poverty or
15 with limited-English proficiency, and the dropout rate.
16   No school district with less than three high schools may
17 establish more than one academy until it has operated the
18 existing academy successfully for two years. No school
19 district with more than two high schools may establish
20 more than two academies until it has operated the
21 existing academy or academies successfully for two years.
22 The years in which districts receive planning grants
23 pursuant to subdivision (a) of Section 54691 shall not be
24 considered years of operation for purposes of this article.
25   SEC. 7.   Section 54694 of the Education Code is
26 repealed.
27   SEC. 8.   Section 54694 is added to the Education Code,
28 to read:
29   54694.   The Superintendent of Public Instruction shall
30 develop guidelines with respect to the Partnership
31 Academies. The guidelines shall include, but not be
32 limited to, enrollment provisions, application procedures,
33 and student eligibility.
34   SEC. 9.   Section 54695 is added to the Education Code,
35 to read:
36   54695.   (a) The ninth grade teachers and counselors
37 in schools maintained by school districts approved to
38 operate academies pursuant to this article shall identify
39 students eligible to participate in a Partnership Academy.
40   (b) Teachers and counselors in schools maintained by

1 school districts approved to operate academies pursuant
2 to this article, business representatives, and academy
3 students of academies that are operating in the area shall
4 be encouraged to make presentations to prospective
5 students and their parents.
6   (c) The staff of each Partnership Academy shall select
7 students from among those who have expressed an
8 interest in the academy and whose parents or guardians
9 have approved the student's participation.
10   SEC. 10.   Section 54696 is added to the Education
11 Code, to read:
12   54696.   The Superintendent of Public Instruction shall
13 contract for a three-year independent review of the
14 effectiveness of the Partnership Academies, and shall
15 report the results of the review to the Legislature by
16 January 1, 1991.
17   The independent review shall include, but not be
18 limited to, the following:
19   (a) An analysis of the extent and degree of success of
20 business and industry involvement, including in-kind
21 contributions, mentor services, summer jobs, and
22 assistance in job placement.
23   (b) The number of pupils entering advanced training
24 programs, obtaining employment, and enrolling in
25 postsecondary institutions.
26   (c) Attendance rates.
27   (d) The number of pupils completing their high
28 school education and graduating.
29   SEC. 11.   (a) There is hereby appropriated from the
30 General Fund to the State Department of Education the
31 sum of ~~six hundred thirty/five thousand dollars ($635,000)~~
32 *five hundred thirty-five thousand dollars ($535,000)* for
33 the 1987–88 fiscal year for allocation in accordance with
34 the following schedule:
35
36 (1) In augmentation to Budget Item
37   6100-166-001 of the 1987 Budget Act,
38   for funding the two school districts
39   which received 1986–87 planning
40   grants... $135,000

1 (2) In augmentation of Budget Item
2   6100-166-001 of the Budget Act, for
3   funding the existing 10 academies
4   pursuant to Section 54691 of the
5   Education Code .... ~~175,000~~
6   *75,000*
7 (3) For the planning grants to 15
8   academies pursuant to Section
9   54691 of the Education Code 225,000
10 (4) For the independent evaluation
11   pursuant to Section 54695 of the
12   Education Code 50,000
13 (5) For the State Department of
14   Education administrative costs for
15   the purposes of Article 5
16   (commencing with Section 54690)
17   of Chapter 9 of Part 29 of the
18   Education Code 50,000
19
20   (b) It is the intent of the Legislature that funding in
21 future fiscal years for the Partnership Academies
22 program, established in Article 5 (commencing with
23 Section 54690) of Chapter 9 of Part 29 of the Education
24 Code, be provided in the annual Budget Act. It is further
25 the intent of the Legislature that the Superintendent of
26 Public Instruction shall include a line item for
27 Partnership Academies in the superintendent's annual
28 budget report to the Governor and the Legislature.

O

References

Academy for Educational Development. *Employment and Educational Experiences of Academy of Finance Graduates.* New York: Academy for Educational Development, 1990.

Alsalam, N., and Rogers, G. T. *The Condition of Education.* Vol. 2: *Postsecondary Education.* NCES 91-638. Washington, D.C.: National Center for Education Statistics, U.S. Department of Education, 1991.

American Association of Community and Junior Colleges. *Program Description Questionnaire for PACE Program at Tri-County Technical College.* Pendleton, S.C.: AACJC National Tech-Prep Clearinghouse, 1989.

Bishop, J. "Occupational Training in High School: When Does It Pay Off?" *Economics of Education Review,* 1989a, *8*(1), 1–15.

Bishop, J. "Why the Apathy in American High Schools?" *Educational Researcher,* 1989b, *18*(1), 6–10.

Bottoms, G., and Presson, A. *Improving General and Vocational Education in High Schools.* Atlanta, Ga.: Southern Regional Education Board, 1989.

Brown, J. S., Collins, A., and Duguid, P. "Situated Cognition and the Culture of Learning." *Educational Researcher,* 1989, *18*(1), 32–41.

Burtless, G., and Orr, L. "Are Classical Experiments Needed for Manpower Policy?" *Journal of Human Resources,* 1986, *21*(4), 606–638.

Center on Organization and Restructuring of Schools. *1992 Information Packet*. Madison: Wisconsin Center for Educational Research, School of Education, University of Wisconsin, 1992.

Committee for Economic Development. *Investing in Our Children*. New York: Committee for Economic Development, 1985.

Dayton, C., Hurdy, L., Schneyer, R., and Kelley, M. (eds.). *California Partnership Academies Resource Guide (1989)*. Palo Alto, Calif.: Stanford Mid-Peninsula Urban Coalition, 1989.

Dayton, C., and Stern, D. *Graduate Follow-up Survey of the June 1988 Graduates of the California Partnership Academies*. Berkeley: Policy Analysis for California Education, University of California, 1990.

Dayton, C., and Stern, D. *Follow-up Survey of the June 1988 and June 1989 Graduates of the California Partnership Academies*. Berkeley: Policy Analysis for California Education, University of California, 1991.

Dayton, C., Weisberg, A., and Stern, D. *California Partnership Academies, 1987–88 Evaluation Report*. Berkeley: Policy Analysis for California Education, University of California, 1989.

Dayton, C., Weisberg, A., Stern, D., and Evans, J. *Peninsula Academies Replications: 1986–87 Evaluation Report*. Berkeley: Policy Analysis for California Education, University of California, 1987.

Dertouzos, M. L., Lester, R. K., and Solow, R. M. *Made in America*. Cambridge, Mass.: MIT Press, 1989.

District of Columbia Public Schools. *The High School Academy Program: Creating Schools of Distinction in Our Nation's Capital*. Concept paper, n.d.

Dornsife, C. *Site Report*. Unpublished document, National Center for Research in Vocational Education, University of California, Berkeley, 1990.

Gamoran, A., and Berends, M. "The Effects of Stratification in Secondary Schools: Synthesis of Survey and Ethnographic Research." *Review of Educational Research*, 1987, *57*(4), 415–435.

Gamoran, A., and Mare, R. D. "Secondary School Tracking and Educational Inequality: Compensation, Reinforcement, or Neutrality?" *American Journal of Sociology,* 1989, *94*(5), 1146–1183.

Goodlad, J. *A Place Called School: Prospects for the Future.* New York: McGraw-Hill, 1984.

Grubb, W. N. "Preparing Youth for Work: The Dilemmas of Education and Training Programs." In D. Stern and D. Eichorn (eds.), *Adolescence and Work: Influences of Social Structure, Labor Markets, and Culture.* Hillsdale, N.J.: Erlbaum, 1989.

Grubb, W. N., and others. *"The Cunning Hand, the Cultured Mind": Models for Integrating Vocational and Academic Education.* Berkeley: National Center for Research in Vocational Education, University of California, 1991.

Guthrie, J. G., and others. *Conditions of Education in California, 1988.* Berkeley: Policy Analysis for California Education, University of California, 1988.

Guthrie, L. F., Guthrie, G. P., and van Heusden, S. *Providing Options for At-Risk Youth: The Health and Media Academies in Oakland. Final Report.* San Francisco: Far West Laboratory for Educational Research and Development, 1990.

Hamilton, S. F. *Apprenticeship for Adulthood.* New York: Free Press, 1990.

Harris, L., and Associates. "Poll on Young People's Skills." *San Francisco Chronicle,* Sept. 30, 1991, p. A3.

Hayward, B. J., Tallmadge, G. K., and Leu, D. J. *Evaluation of Dropout Prevention and Reentry Demonstration Projects in Vocational Education. Final Report: Phase II (Revised Draft).* Research Triangle Park, N.C.: Research Triangle Institute, 1991.

Hinds, M. de C. "Cutting the Dropout Rate: High Goal, but Low Hopes." *New York Times,* Feb. 17, 1990, pp. 1, 11.

Illinois State Board of Education. *Illinois Tech-prep: Preparing Students for the Twenty-first Century.* Springfield: Illinois State Board of Education, 1990.

Kazis, R. *Toward Defining Workable Models for Youth Apprenticeship.* Somerville, Mass.: Jobs for the Future, 1991.

Kearns, D. T., and Doyle, D. P. *Winning the Brain Race: A Bold Plan to Make Our Schools Competitive.* San Francisco: Institute for Contemporary Studies Press, 1988.

LaLonde, R. J. "Evaluating the Econometric Evaluation of Training Programs with Experimental Data." *American Economic Review,* 1986, *65*(4), 604–620.

Lave, J., and Wenger, E. *Situated Learning, Legitimate Peripheral Participation.* Cambridge, England: Cambridge University Press, 1991.

Lazerson, M., and Grubb, W. N. *American Education and Vocationalism: A Documentary History.* New York: Teachers College Press, 1974.

Maddala, G. S. *Limited-dependent and Qualitative Variables in Econometrics.* New York: Cambridge University Press, 1983.

Mitchell, V., Russell, E. S., and Benson, C. *Exemplary Urban Career-oriented Secondary School Programs.* Berkeley: National Center for Research in Vocational Education, University of California, 1989.

National Academy Foundation. Informational materials. New York: National Academy Foundation, 1991a.

National Academy Foundation. "Pilot Academy Programs Complete Successful First Year." *NAF Bulletin,* 1991b, *1*(1), 3.

National Academy of Sciences, Panel on Secondary School Education and the Changing Workplace. *High Schools and the Changing Workplace: The Employers' View.* Washington, D.C.: National Academy Press, 1984.

National Alliance of Business. *Who Will Do the Work? A Business Guide for Preparing Tomorrow's Workforce.* Washington, D.C.: National Alliance of Business, 1989.

National Center on Education and the Economy. *America's Choice: High Skills or Low Wages!* Report of the Commission on the Skills of the American Workforce. Rochester, N.Y.: National Center on Education and the Economy, 1990.

National Commission on Excellence in Education. *A Nation at Risk: The Imperative for Education Reform.* Washington, D.C.: U.S. Department of Education, 1983.

National Institute of Education. *The Vocational Education Study: The Final Report.* Washington, D.C.: National Institute of Education, 1981.

Neubauer, A. "Philadelphia High School Academies." *Educational Horizons,* 1986, *65*(1), 16–19.

Newmann, F. M. *Final Report: National Center on Effective Secondary Schools.* Madison: School of Education, University of Wisconsin, 1991.

Oakes, J. "Limiting Opportunity: Students' Race and Curricular Differences in Secondary Vocational Education." *American Journal of Education,* 1983, *91,* 328–355.

Oakes, J. *Keeping Track: How Schools Structure Inequality.* New Haven, Conn.: Yale University Press, 1985.

Ogle, L. T., Alsalam, N., and Rogers, G. T. *The Condition of Education.* Vol. 1: *Elementary and Secondary Education.* NCES 91-637. Washington, D.C.: National Center for Education Statistics, U.S. Department of Education, 1991.

Parnell, D. *The Neglected Majority.* Alexandria, Va.: American Association of Community and Junior Colleges, 1985.

Parnell, D. "Why Applied Academics?" *The Balance Sheet,* South-Western Publishing, Fall 1990, pp. 12–14.

Philadelphia High School Academies, Inc. *Around the Academies.* Newsletter. Philadelphia: Philadelphia High School Academies, Inc.

Philadelphia High School Academies, Inc. Publicity packet. Philadelphia: Philadelphia High School Academies, Inc., 1991.

Psacharopoulos, G. "To Vocationalize or Not to Vocationalize? That Is the Curriculum Question." *International Review of Education,* 1987, *33*(2), 187–211.

Raizen, S. A. *Reforming Education for Work: A Cognitive Science Perspective.* Berkeley: National Center for Research in Vocational Education, University of California, 1989.

Reller, D. J. *The Peninsula Academies: Final Technical Evaluation Report.* Palo Alto, Calif.: American Institutes for Research in the Behavioral Sciences, 1984.

Reller, D. J. *The Peninsula Academies: Interim Evaluation*

Report, 1984–85 School Year. Palo Alto, Calif.: American Institutes for Research in the Behavioral Sciences, 1985.

Reller, D. J. *A Longitudinal Study of the Graduates of the Peninsula Academies: Final Report.* Palo Alto, Calif.: American Institutes for Research in the Behavioral Sciences, 1987.

Resnick, L. B. *Education and Learning to Think.* Washington, D.C.: National Academy Press, 1987a.

Resnick, L. B. "Learning in School and Out." *Educational Researcher,* 1987b, *16,* 13–20.

Rosenbaum, J. E. "Empowering Schools and Teachers: A New Link to Jobs for the Non-college Bound." In Commission on Workforce Quality and Labor Market Efficiency, U.S. Department of Labor, *Investing in People: A Strategy to Address America's Workforce Crisis.* Background Papers, Vol. 1. Washington, D.C.: U.S. Department of Labor, 1989.

Rosenbaum, J. E., and Kariya, T. "Do School Achievements Affect the Early Jobs of High School Graduates in the United States and Japan?" *Sociology of Education,* 1991, *64,* 78–95.

Rubin, V., Gibson, K., and Stern, D. *Support of Academies in the Oakland Public Schools by the Oakland Redevelopment Agency: Final Report for the Evaluation of the Second Year.* Berkeley: University-Oakland Metropolitan Forum, University of California, 1992.

Schmidt, P. "Foundation Formed to Spur Partnerships to Create Business-School 'Academies.'" *Education Week,* Nov. 22, 1989, p. 5.

Sinclair, M. "Academy Students Learn What Makes D.C. Work." *The Washington Post,* June 12, 1991, p. B3.

Sizer, T. R. *Horace's Compromise.* Boston: Houghton Mifflin, 1984.

Sizer, T. R. *Horace's School.* Boston: Houghton Mifflin, 1991.

Snyder, P., and McMullan, B. J. *Allies in Education: A Profile of Philadelphia High School Academies, Philadelphia, Pennsylvania.* Philadelphia: Public/Private Ventures, 1987a.

Snyder, P., and McMullan, B. J. *Allies in Education: Schools and Businesses Working Together for At-Risk Youth.* Philadelphia: Public/Private Ventures, 1987b.

South Mountain Community College. *ACE (Achieving a College Education).* Phoenix, Ariz.: South Mountain Community College, 1989.

Steinberg, L. *Adverse Impact of Part-time Employment on Adolescent Schooling and Behavior: Replication and Elaboration.* Philadelphia: Center for Research in Human Development and Education, Temple University, 1989.

Stern, D. *Combining School and Work: Options in High Schools and Two-year Colleges.* Washington, D.C.: Office of Vocational and Adult Education, U.S. Department of Education, 1991.

Stern, D., Dayton, C., Paik, I., and Weisberg, A. "Benefits and Costs of Dropout Prevention in a High School Program Combining Academic and Vocational Education: Third-year Results from Replications of the California Peninsula Academies." *Educational Evaluation and Policy Analysis,* 1989, *11*(4), 405–416.

Stern, D., Paik, I., Catterall, J. S., and Nakata, Y. "Labor Market Experience of Teenagers with and Without High School Diplomas." *Economics of Education Review,* 1989, *8*(3), 233–246.

Stern, D., and others. "Combining Academic and Vocational Courses in an Integrated Program to Reduce High School Dropout Rates: Second-year Results from Replications of the California Peninsula Academies." *Educational Evaluation and Policy Analysis,* 1988, *10*(2), 161–170.

Stone, J. "Classic Community Service by Public Servants." *The Bureaucrat,* Summer 1990, pp. 8–10.

Stone, J. R. III, Stern, D., Hopkins, C., and McMillion, M. "Adolescents' Perception of Their Work: School Supervised and Non-School Supervised." *Journal of Vocational Education Research,* 1990, *15*(2), 31–53.

Task Force on Youth Employment, Wisconsin Department of Public Instruction. *Final Recommendations of the State Superintendent's Task Force on Youth Employment.* Madison: Wisconsin Department of Public Instruction, 1990.

U.S. Congress. *Act to Provide for the Promotion of Vocational Education* [later called the Smith-Hughes Act]. 64th Cong., 2nd sess., 1917.

U.S. Congress. *Carl D. Perkins Vocational and Applied Technology Education Act Amendments of 1990.* 101st Cong., 2nd sess., 1990.

U.S. Department of Education. *America 2000: An Education Strategy.* Washington, D.C.: Government Printing Office, 1991.

U.S. Department of Labor, Secretary's Commission on Achieving Necessary Skills. *What Work Requires of Schools.* Washington, D.C.: Government Printing Office, 1991.

U.S. General Accounting Office. *School Dropouts: Survey of Local Programs.* GAO/HRD-87-108. Washington, D.C.: Government Printing Office, 1987.

Wehlage, G. G., and others. *Reducing the Risk: Schools as Communities of Support.* Philadelphia: Falmer Press, 1989.

Whitehead, A. N. *The Aims of Education.* New York: Macmillan, 1929.

Wolf, D., Bixby, J., Glenn, J., and Gardner, H. "To Use Their Minds Well: Investigating New Forms of Student Assessment." *Review of Research in Education,* 1991, *17,* 31–74.

Index

❧ ○ ❧

A

AB 3104, 41-42, 43, 44

Academic Learning Integrating Vocational Education (ALIVE), 144-146

Academic rigor, 11-12; in career academies, 21, 38-39. *See also* Academics

Academics, combined with technical training, 11-12, 15, 17, 18-19, 152-155. *See also* Academic rigor; Career academies; Vocational education

Academies. *See* Career academies

Academy for Educational Development (AED), 60, 66, 69

Academy movement, evolution of, 32-55; and unification, 54-55. *See also* Career academies

Academy of applied automotive and mechanical sciences, 34. *See also* Philadelphia Academies

Achieving College Education (ACE), 157

Agribusiness employers, 107

Aides, instructional, 80-81, 126-127. *See also* Staffing; Teachers; Technical assistants

ALIVE. *See* Academic Learning Integrating Vocational Education

Allison, J., 46

Alsalam, N., 4, 10

America 2000, 159-160, 161-162

American Achievement Tests, 162

American Association of Community and Junior Colleges, 156, 157, 159

American Express Company: and NAF academy of finance, 32, 46-48; and NAF academy of travel and tourism, 48

American Institutes for Research, 57

America's Choice: High Skills or Low Wages! (National Center on Education and the Economy), 3, 143, 160

The Andromeda Strain, 20

Apathy, of students, 6. *See also* Motivation

Assessment, student, 20, 127, 128, 162-163

At-risk students, 15, 41, 43, 128, 149; developing curriculum for, 90; jobs as motivation to, 100; and peer group pressure, 96; staffing for, 79-80; success of, 131; targeting of, 23-24

Average daily attendance (ADA) funding, 29. *See also* Funding

Aviation High School (New York), 154